D0856619

CLASSIC AMERICAN WRITERS

Edith Wharton

RICHARD WORTH

JULIAN ⓜ MESSNER
Published by Simon & Schuster

New York   London   Toronto   Sydney   Tokyo   Singapore

Photo Acknowledgments:
Page v: Museum of the City of New York, The Byron Collection.
Page 8: The Beinecke Rare Book and Manuscript Library, Yale University.
Page 13: The Beinecke Rare Book and Manuscript Library, Yale University.
Page 16: The New York Public Library Picture Collection.
Page 22: The New-York Historical Society.
Page 27: The Beinecke Rare Book and Manuscript Library, Yale University.
Page 32: The Beinecke Rare Book and Manuscript Library, Yale University.
Page 35: The Bettmann Archive.
Page 48: Museum of the City of New York, The Byron Collection.
Page 55: The Beinecke Rare Book and Manuscript Library, Yale University.
Page 82: Museum of the City of New York, The Byron Collection.
Page 96: The New York Public Library Picture Collection.
Page 103: The New York Public Library Picture Collection.
Page 112: The Beinecke Rare Book and Manuscript Library, Yale University.
Page 129: The Beinecke Rare Book and Manuscript Library, Yale University.

JULIAN MESSNER
Published by Simon & Schuster
1230 Avenue of the Americas,
New York, New York 10020
Copyright © 1994 by Richard Worth

All rights reserved including the right of reproduction in whole or in
part in any form.

JULIAN MESSNER and colophon are trademarks of Simon & Schuster
Designed by Virginia Pope.
Manufactured in the United States of America.

10 9 8 7 6 5 4 3 2 1

Library of Congress Cataloging-in-Publication Data
Worth, Richard.
    Edith Wharton / by Richard Worth.
        p.   cm. — (Classic American writers)
    Includes bibliographical references (p.) and index.
    1. Wharton, Edith, 1862–1937—Juvenile literature.   2. Authors,
American—20th century—Biography—Juvenile literature.
[1. Wharton, Edith, 1862–1937.   2. Authors, American.]   I. Title.
II. Series.   PS3545.H16Z944   1994   813'.52—dc20   [B]   93-23207
CIP   AC

ISBN: 0-671-86615-X

CONTENTS

1 ... In Old New York ... 1

2 ... Coming of Age ... 11

3 ... A Writer Emerges ... 21

4 ... The Mount ... 31

5 ... *The House of Mirth* ... 43

6 ... Teddy Wharton and Morton Fullerton ... 53

7 ... *Ethan Frome* ... 63

8 ... Endings and Beginnings ... 71

9 ... *The Reef* ... 75

10 ... *The Custom of the Country* ... 81

11 ... War! ... 91

12 ... *The Age of Innocence* ... 101

13 ... Transitions and the Writer's Art ... 111

14 ... *Hudson River Bracketed* ... 121

15 ... The Final Years ... 127

16 ... The Immortality of Edith Wharton ... 133

NOTES ... 137

CHRONOLOGY ... 145

FURTHER READING ... 147

INDEX ... 149

Fifth Avenue near Central Park in the late 1890s. By this time, the Avenue had become the favored residence for New York City's wealthiest families.

1

IN OLD
NEW YORK

In 1860, the dashing eighteen-year-old Prince of Wales, heir to the British throne, came to North America. Stopping briefly in Canada, he traveled south to New York City for a visit that was immediately hailed as the most important social event in the city's history. New Yorkers, who had always considered theirs to be the most important city in the United States, now congratulated themselves that they had been right all along. Why else would the future Edward VII grace New York City with his presence?

On the day of his arrival, a crowd estimated at 100,000 people lined Broadway to catch a glimpse of the royal heir. The diarist George Templeton Strong, a member of New York's social elite, sat on the reception committee that had planned the festivities for the prince's visit. He described the throng as "one long dense mass of impatient humanity. All windows on either side were filled. Temporary platforms crowded, at five dollars a seat. . . . What a spectacle-loving people we are!"[1]

Following the prince's triumphant procession up Broadway, he was taken to the Fifth Avenue Hotel at Twenty-third Street, a new six-story structure that boasted the first elevator and the first rooms with private baths of any hotel in the United States. Later, the prince attended a reception in his honor at Trinity Church, followed by a gala evening of entertainment at the Academy of Music. Located on Fourteenth Street, the academy was the city's only opera house and the exclusive preserve of the wealthy, where box seats were literally handed down from one generation to the next.

The ball began at 10:00 P.M., the common starting time for such events in that period. The prince proved tireless as he waltzed and polkaed with every woman who found herself fortunate enough to have a turn with him. He seemed to move effortlessly among the hundreds of other dancers—men in their formal evening attire and women in magnificent low-cut gowns with voluminous hoop skirts that swayed across the floor. After leaving for a dinner backstage at the academy with New York's governor and the city's mayor, the prince returned and continued dancing until 4:30 in the morning. His presence left an indelible mark on everyone who attended, and Strong, who had been given the privilege of shaking hands with the heir to the British throne, remarked in his diary: "I think of having my right-hand glove framed and glazed with an appropriate inscription."[2]

The visit of the Prince of Wales symbolized New Yorkers' impressionability and their feelings of close kinship to Europe and things European. News from Great Britain and the Continent reached New York ahead of any other American city. British author Charles Dickens had begun his American speaking tour in New York, and in 1850 the famous Swedish singer Jenny Lind had made her American debut at Castle Garden, a huge auditorium on the tip of Manhattan Island. A few years later, Castle Garden was converted into an entry point for the multitude of immigrants who sailed to America from Europe each year. Over 100,000 men, women, and children arrived in 1860 alone. At Castle Garden, they converted their native currency to American dollars, bought clothing and food from one of the many street vendors, and often arranged passage out West. But many immigrants stayed behind, swelling the population of the city.

In 1860, the population of greater New York had passed the one-million mark. It was considered the business and cultural center of the United States. Ships crowded into New York's harbor—tall-masted schooners with their billowing sails and steamboats with their huge paddle-wheels—bringing valuable cargo, as well as the lowly and the highborn from other parts of America, Europe, and the Far East. Plying their way across the harbors, ferryboats transported commuters from Brooklyn, Staten Island, or New Jersey. Others walked to work from their homes inside the city or rode in omnibuses, covered horse-drawn vehicles that were crowded with passengers.

Many of these people worked on Wall Street, the nation's financial hub and home of the New York Stock Exchange. Or they stood behind the wooden counters of the department stores along Broadway, the city's most fashionable shopping area. Each morning the carriages of New York's finest families would roll along Broadway and pull up in front of the doors of the city's most exclusive emporiums. A liveried footman would then step down from each carriage and usher his wealthy employers through the double-storied portals. Inside, the well-to-do could outfit themselves with the latest in Parisian clothing and the finest jewelry or choose from the most expensive decorations for their homes.

Many of these homes were located around Fifth Avenue, in the lower part of Manhattan, between Washington Square and

Madison Square. They were stately, solidly built, rather unimaginative brownstones, which perfectly matched the stolid, very conservative nature of their occupants. These were among the oldest families in New York—the Schermerhorns, Brevoorts, Stuyvesants, Stevenses, Joneses, Gallatins, Rhinelanders, and Ledyards. Their substantial wealth flowed largely from the rents on New York real estate that had been passed down through their families for generations. Some of this land contained the dreary tenement buildings where the city's immigrants were forced to live in squalor, but the wealthy rarely troubled themselves with such unpleasant thoughts.

Since neither the men nor the women of these old families needed to work, they could arise late and enjoy a leisurely breakfast prepared by a cook and placed before them by one of their household servants. After breakfast men might go off to one of the many clubs that had sprung up in the city—the Manhattan Club, the Knickerbocker Club, or the Union League Club. Indeed, they might spend the entire day there reading and visiting with their friends. Or they might decide to go horseback riding in the new Central Park, which was currently under construction.

Designed by Frederick Law Olmsted and Calvert Vaux, work on this 840-acre site in the center of Manhattan began in 1857. The park was crisscrossed by hundreds of footpaths, carriage drives, and bridle paths—all magnificently landscaped with beautiful shade trees. A large mall was constructed with a bandstand at one end, and on warm summer days chairs were set out under striped awnings along the mall where people would sit comfortably and listen to band music. At one end of the mall, couples promenaded under a trellised walkway over-looking an artificial lake that had been created in the park. Boating on the lake was extremely popular during the summer, as boat rentals were made available from the boathouses located along the shore. During the winter the lake became a huge skating rink. Men in high hats and women in fur-trimmed coats glided across the ice, while along the shore couples in sleighs raced across the snow behind teams of sturdy horses.

During the day Central Park was the playground of the wealthy, because they were the only ones who had the free time and could afford the carriages, or the sleighs, or the boat rentals. In the evenings, the well-to-do could often be found at the theater, attending the opera at the Academy of Music, enjoying elaborate balls, or at home giving sumptuous dinner parties for their friends.

Women would plan these dinners with the help of their servants weeks in advance. Engraved, formal invitations would be sent out, usually to the same select group of couples who made up their social circles. On the day of the dinner party, the women might spend several hours dressing, since there was frequently little else to do. Guests arrived at 8:00 P.M., traded polite conversation in the drawing room, and then went into dinner.

The dinners themselves always consisted of a succession of rich dishes—soups, salads, beef, poultry, and dessert—following one after the other well into the evening. Since dining was a primary form of entertainment among the upper classes, there was no reason to hurry, and people often lingered at the table for several hours. Then at the appointed time, the hostess would rise from her position at the head of the table and lead the other ladies into the drawing room, leaving the men behind to enjoy their cigars, coffee, and Madeira wine while they talked "business." After the men had finished, they would rejoin the ladies for "polite" conversation.

Among the social elite of old New York, one couple who had gained a reputation for their fine dinner parties were George Frederic and Lucretia Rhinelander Jones of West Twenty-third Street. Between them, the Joneses were related to many of the city's oldest families. During the American Revolution, Lucretia's grandfather, Major General Ebenezer Stevens, fought at Bunker Hill. Two years later he helped turn the tide of battle at Saratoga, and late in the war he participated in the campaign that led to the surrender of Britain's General Cornwallis at Yorktown. Following the war, Stevens had grown rich in the East India trade and built a home for himself on Long Island, which he called The Mount. He also saw to it that his eleven children married Schermerhorns, Gallatins, and Rhinelanders.

Nevertheless, the Rhinelander fortune began to decline in the next generation, and as Lucretia was growing up she was known as one of the "poor Rhinelander girls." She was "poor," however, only in relation to some of her wealthier cousins. But it was enough of a problem for George Frederic Jones's widowed mother, Elizabeth Schermerhorn Jones, to express some disapproval when her son began courting the young Lucretia.

However, George Frederic would not be put off. He would steal out of the family mansion on Long Island Sound and make his way down to the water where he kept a rowboat. With wooden oars as a makeshift mast, he rigged a sail out of an old quilt and set out along the water for secret meetings with Lucretia. Eventually, in 1844 the couple were married.

Like many of their wealthy contemporaries, the Joneses traveled extensively in Europe after their marriage. They were in Paris in 1848, for example, where they saw the portly French monarch, Louis Philippe, and his queen flee into exile during the revolution. When they weren't in Europe or New

York, the Joneses lived at Pencraig, their home in Newport, Rhode Island. Newport was a favorite summer resort of New York's upper classes, although the homes built there during the 1840s and 1850s were far more modest than the sprawling mansions that would be constructed several decades later by the Astors and the Vanderbilts.

Fairly early in their marriage the Joneses had two sons. Then in January 1862, twelve years after her last child was born, Lucretia gave birth to a daughter. The couple christened the little girl Edith Newbold Jones.

In her autobiography, *A Backward Glance,* Edith Wharton wrote that her first memory was as a child of three when she went walking with her father on a cold winter's day up Fifth Avenue. Along each side of the street stood an imposing line of brownstones and an occasional open plot of land where cows still grazed. As Edith and her father trudged northward, they approached the Forty-second Street reservoir—a huge stone structure that provided drinking water to the city's inhabitants. To keep the bitter weather at bay, Edith had been carefully dressed in a white satin bonnet and a wool veil, "a gossamer veil of the finest white Shetland wool."[3]

The first winter of Edith's memory also proved to be the last of the tumultuous conflict that had divided the nation for four terrible years—the Civil War. Edith did not mention the war in her autobiography, nor do we know whether her parents were among the thousands who witnessed the funeral procession of assassinated President Abraham Lincoln, which rolled slowly through New York City shortly after the war ended.

However, the completion of the war did have a significant impact on the Joneses' lifestyle. Real estate values began to decline, and George Frederic saw the income from his land holdings drop noticeably. Therefore, he decided to lease his

Edith Newbold Jones at about age eight. Edith spent the early years of her childhood living in Europe.

home in New York City, as well as his summer residence in Newport, and move to Europe, where the family could live more cheaply.

The Joneses traveled to Rome, where Edith played along the steps of the Roman Forum, visited the ruins of ancient villas, and walked on the Appian Way. The family's journey then took them bumping along the backroads of Spain to the quiet pools and gardens of the magnificent Moorish palace of the Alhambra in Granada, and to Seville on the Guadalquivir

River where Spanish galleons had embarked for the Americas in the days when Spain still ruled a rich empire.

Eventually the Joneses settled in Paris, the city that would become Edith's favorite. Although she was not yet old enough to read, Edith recalled walking around her home pretending to read aloud from Washington Irving's *The Alhambra*, making up stories from her imagination. Her parents became concerned that Edith was spending too much time alone and wanted her to go out and play with other children. "But I did not want them to intrude on my privacy," she wrote. "What I really preferred was to be alone with Washington Irving and my dream."[4]

Finally, George Frederic taught Edith the alphabet, and gradually she became absorbed in reading some of the books in her father's library. But her blissful childhood days were suddenly interrupted. In 1870, while her family was staying briefly outside of Paris, Edith was stricken with typhoid fever, a disease that often proved fatal. Although she fully recovered, the Joneses decided not to return to Paris because war had broken out between France and Prussia. Instead, they moved to Florence. Here Edith began to learn Italian from a private tutor, having already picked up some German from one of the governesses that her parents had engaged to help them take care of her. The Joneses would remain in Italy until 1872, when they finally sailed home to America.

2

COMING OF AGE

Some of Edith's fondest memories as a child were of Pencraig, her family's home in Newport where they spent the summer after their return from Paris. The house had a huge veranda where a ten-year-old could sit and daydream on a sultry afternoon. There was a flowered meadow to play in, a pony to ride, a garden with tart strawberries and sweet pears to eat, and a private cove for swimming. Edith also accompanied her parents to Newport lawn parties, and with a keen eye began to observe all that was going on at them. Archery had become the rage among the fashionable set, and young women with long dresses and hats with heavy veils to keep out the sun (no one wanted to mar a creamy complexion with a suntan) would line up in front of the targets to show off their skills. Only at the last moment, as each woman was ready to take aim, would she lift her veil, line up the shot, and then release the bowstring, sending a sleek arrow toward its destination.

These statuesque archers became heroines in the early stories that Edith wrote while she was still a child. Years later she vividly recalled showing the first of these efforts to her mother:

> *My first attempt (at the age of eleven) was a novel, which*
> *began: "Oh, how do you do, Mrs. Brown?" said Mrs.*
> *Tompkins. "If only I had known you were going to call I*
> *should have tidied up the drawing-room." Timourously, I*
> *submitted this to my mother, and never shall I forget the sud-*
> *den drop of my creative frenzy when she returned with the icy*
> *comment: "Drawing-rooms are always tidy."*[1]

While Edith may have been momentarily put off by her mother's reaction, she was hardly discouraged enough to stop writing and continued to turn out poems and stories regularly throughout her childhood. When she was about fifteen, Edith wrote a short novel—a love story set among the European upper classes. She always prided herself on writing about "real people," by which Edith meant adults. Once Edith even summoned the courage to send one of her poems to a New York City newspaper, which decided it was good enough to print. Another of her poems appeared in the prestigious *Atlantic Monthly,* after it was submitted by none other than Henry Wadsworth Longfellow, who was a friend of one of Edith's neighbors. In 1878, a collection of her verses was privately printed in Newport, probably arranged with the help of her parents.

Nevertheless, Edith's parents had mixed feelings about her literary efforts. They were people who insisted on correct English and had a keen ear for the English language, a talent their daughter inherited:

> *I used to say that I had been taught only two things in my*
> *childhood: the modern languages and good manners. . . . But*
> *in justice to my parents I ought to have named a third element*
> *in my training: a reverence for the English language as spoken*

The teenaged Edith just before her presentation to New York society.

according to the best usage. . . . My parents' ears were
wounded by an unsuitable word as those of the musical are
hurt by a false note.[2]

However, the Joneses were certainly not literary people. At the quiet dinners they routinely hosted, the conversation usually turned to real estate or country homes, the opera, or the latest fashions from Europe. Literature was hardly considered an interesting topic of discussion. In fact, writers (with only a few exceptions such as a family friend like Washington Irving) were not even members of the Joneses' social circle. They were considered odd and different, and a woman writer was considered the oddest of all.

Women of Edith's social standing were expected to marry and have children. Steps had to be taken to find a suitable husband. The first such step was for a young woman's mother to arrange a coming-out party. All the members of a girl's social set would be present for her formal introduction to society and announcement of eligibility. While these parties were frequently held at a posh restaurant, like Delmonico's on Fifth Avenue, Mrs. Jones preferred that Edith have her coming out at the home of Mrs. Levi Morton, one of the few women in New York City with a house large enough for a ballroom that could accommodate many guests.

So Edith Jones was presented to New York society. She was seventeen years old with striking red hair and large, pensive brown eyes. Despite these attributes Edith was not considered a beauty. She didn't dazzle, and perhaps more seriously, she was shy and bookish, qualities not looked upon as desirable in a young society wife. Nevertheless, Edith managed to live through that memorable evening in 1879 and formally entered a new stage of her life.

Since the end of the Civil War, New York society had slowly been changing. The old, established families— represented by the Rhinelanders, Joneses, and their kind— were being forced to give way to the newly rich. Some of the nouveaux riches had made their millions providing supplies to the Union army, others participated in the economic boom that followed the war, while still others had amassed fortunes even earlier—not early enough, however, to satisfy the old moneyed classes of New York. John Jacob Astor, for example, had made himself fabulously wealthy by building a fur-trading monopoly in the early part of the nineteenth century, and Cornelius Vanderbilt had done the same thing a few decades later in shipping and railroads. But the wealth was too new and the way it had been acquired—by business and financial deal-ings that were not always strictly honest—was too crass to appeal to New York's traditional elite. The old elite also resented the way nouveaux riches families constantly displayed their wealth. As Edith's mother had always told her: "Never talk about money, and think about it as little as possible."[3]

Nevertheless, the newly rich were impossible to ignore. Financiers like Vanderbilt, William Backhouse Astor, August Belmont and Leonard Jerome were building opulent homes along upper Fifth Avenue and Madison Avenue, driving their magnificent carriages through Central Park, and shopping at all the most fashionable stores. Most importantly, they were clamoring to be admitted into the city's high society. The easi-est way to break into high society was through marriage, and the newly rich pursued marriage intently. Belmont broke into society by marrying Caroline Slidell Perry, the daughter of Commodore Matthew Perry who had sailed to Japan, and the niece of Oliver Hazard Perry, the naval hero of the War of 1812. William Backhouse Astor married Caroline Schermer-horn—one of *the* Schermerhorns—who was shortly to

*The wealthy of Edith Wharton's day socialized at dinner parties, vacation resorts, and
most memorably, at lavish balls.*

become *the* Mrs. Astor, acknowledged matriarch of New York
society.

Each winter, the city's social season got under way with a
series of balls, dinner parties, and theater suppers. Attending all
or some of them was the true work of the well-to-do and
socially prominent. True to her class, Edith marked her first
year as a young debutante by making the usual rounds of these
society functions.

The highlight of the season was Mrs. Astor's annual ball
held on the second or third Monday in January. As she did for
all such events, Mrs. Astor would carefully plan the evening
with Ward McAllister, a kind of social prime minister. It was
McAllister who would arrange the menu, the decorations, and
the evening's entertainment. The guest list would only include
society's most elite families; in fact it was McAllister who
coined the phrase "the 400" to describe the number of New
York families who really mattered. According to him, this was

the number of party-goers who could comfortably fit into
Mrs. Astor's ballroom. Guests would begin arriving for the ball
at 11:00 P.M., when they would be received by Mrs. Astor
standing beneath a life-sized portrait of herself. Wearing the
latest creation designed exclusively for her by Worth of Paris,
she was usually covered in jewels—a diamond tiara, a diamond
choker, and a diamond necklace. The ball would continue until
the early morning, with Mrs. Astor sitting on a divan, posi-
tioned on a raised dais at one end of the ballroom, watching
the dancers. Periodically, she would invite one of the assembled women at the ball to share the divan with her and favor
this fortunate person with a few moments of conversation.

Since Edith's father was related to Mrs. Astor, the Joneses
might have been expected to be among the guests for her
annual ball. By 1880, however, George Frederic's health had
declined, and the family returned to Europe hoping that the
climate might help him recover. Arriving in London, the
Joneses traveled south to Nice and Cannes on the French Riviera. While her father rested and tried to recoup his health,
Edith had time to enjoy some of the beauty of the Mediter-
ranean coast. But her father's condition continued to worsen,
and he died in 1882. Looking back many years later, Edith
seemed to believe that there was far more to her father than he
had ever shown the world. He had been born into conservative New York society, and there he remained, content to live
the same way as most of his friends. And yet, she thought, he
might have had the makings of a much different person. As
Edith wrote:

> "I have wondered what stifled cravings had once germinated
> in him, and what manner of man he was really meant to be.
> That he was a lonely one, haunted by something always
> unexpressed and unattained, I am sure."[4]

Upon her father's death, Edith returned with her mother to Pencraig. There life continued much as it had before. Summer days were wiled away with carriage rides, games of lawn tennis, chaperoned dances, and small dinners at the homes of her married friends. All of this was part of a formal mating ritual that brought both sexes together without ever allowing them much chance to be alone with each other, at least until they were married.

According to her biographer, R.W.B. Lewis, Edith became romantically involved during this period. His name was Harry Stevens, and he was a very wealthy young man Edith had seen on numerous occasions in New York and Newport. In fact, the couple were engaged to be married until the prospective bridegroom's mother, Mrs. Paran Stevens, stepped in and forced them to break it off. While it was nothing for parents in this period to interfere with their children when it came to the choice of a marriage partner, it would have been a bitter blow for any young woman and especially for one as shy and self-conscious as Edith.

Of course, there would be other men. In the summer of 1883, while she and her mother were summering in Bar Harbor, Maine, Edith met Walter Van Rensselaer Berry. Studying to be a lawyer, Berry also had a keen appreciation for literature and art, which appealed to Edith, and in fact, she was very much attracted to him. But nothing more serious came of it, although Berry would remain perhaps her closest lifelong friend, as well as her editor.

That same summer, a far more serious relationship began to develop between Edith and Edward Robbins (Teddy) Wharton, who was thirty-three years old and from a well-to-do Boston family. She saw Teddy in Newport, and the following year he was her escort at a ball in New York. Relaxed and easy going, Teddy was similar to many of the men in Edith's social set and must have had a comfortable appeal to her. He had his own income and no need to work or any interest in working. His primary interests were sports—fishing, golf, and hunting. In 1885, they were married.

Following their marriage, Edith and Teddy embarked upon a lifestyle of regular travel that would continue throughout their lives together. During the first years, they lived from June until February on her mother's estate in Newport and the remaining months in Europe, mostly touring Italy. Edith soon realized, if she hadn't already, that Teddy would not provide her with much intellectual companionship. So their journeys often included a third person. A family friend, Egerton Winthrop, many years Edith's senior, took her under his wing and shared with her his broad interest and enthusiasm for art, furniture, and Roman antiquities. While Winthrop would remain a valued friend until his death, Edith always regretted that he never seemed to accomplish very much with his life. He was like so many men she had met who "combined a cultivated taste with marked social gifts. Their weakness was that, save in a few cases, they made so little use of their abilities."[5]

In 1889, the Whartons decided to rent a home on Madison Avenue in New York City. Here Edith began to develop an intellectual circle that she hoped would make up for much that seemed lacking in her marriage. She also began writing poetry again. Edith sent some of her work to three of the leading literary magazines of the day—*Scribner's, Harper's,* and the *Century. Scribner's* magazine decided to publish one of her poems. In 1891, *Scribner's* also published one of her short stories, *Mrs. Mansey's View.* These were the first in a long series of literary works that would appear under the name Edith Wharton.

015 WALTRIP H.S. LIBRARY

3

A WRITER EMERGES

In December 1893, *Scribner's* published another engaging short story by the magazine's new author, Edith Wharton. Titled *The Fullness of Life*, it describes a young woman who goes to heaven following her death. There she encounters the Spirit of Life, who inquires about her marriage:

> *"You were married," said the Spirit, "yet you did not find the fullness of life in your marriage?"*
>
> *"Oh, dear, no," she replied, with an indulgent scorn, "my marriage was a very incomplete affair."*
>
> *"And yet you were fond of your husband?"*
>
> *"You have hit upon the exact word; I was fond of him, yes, as I was fond of my grandmother, and the house that I was born in, and my old nurse. . . . But I have sometimes thought that a woman's nature is like a great house full of rooms: There is the hall, through which everyone passes in going in and out; the drawing room, where one receives formal visits; the sitting room, where the members of the family come and go as they list; but beyond that, far beyond are other*

A portrait of Edith Wharton from 1890. She was in her late twenties.

rooms, the handles of whose doors perhaps are never turned; no one knows the way to them, no one knows whither they lead; and in the innermost room, the holy of holies, the soul sits alone and waits for a footstep that never comes."

"And your husband," asked the Spirit, after a pause, "never got beyond the family sitting room?"

"Never," she returned, impatiently, "and the worst of it was that he was quite content to remain there."[1]

Throughout her long literary career, Edith Wharton would continually lift the curtain that cloaked human relationships to reveal what was really happening between a man and a woman. Frequently, the marriages she described—like the one in *The Fullness of Life*—were filled with emptiness and isolation. And it seemed the woman's lot to suffer most in these unsatisfying relationships because she had hoped for, had expected, so much more. Thus, her own feelings of disappointment and loneliness were so much greater, and she was always more acutely aware of them than her husband. It was a problem that Edith Wharton understood far too well. Only a few years into her marriage to Teddy, Edith was already dissatisfied. *The Fullness of Life* is probably a thinly disguised tale of their relationship.

On the surface, Edith and Teddy Wharton probably appeared perfectly content, much like other couples in their social set who entertained regularly, lived part of the year in New York and part in Newport, with annual trips to Europe. Indeed, Teddy may not have been aware that any problem existed in his marriage. But on a much deeper level, the two were already drifting apart. Edith longed to talk about literature and the arts, and at the Whartons' home in New York City, she had begun to surround herself with a group of men who could provide her with intellectual stimulation. There was Egerton Winthrop, who often accompanied the Whartons on their trips abroad; Ogden Codman, a young Boston architect; Robert Minturn, a linguist; and Bayard Cutting, a wealthy railroad magnate with a magnificent home on Madison Avenue. Teddy, whose main literary interests were newspapers and adventure novels, seems to have found very little to attract him in these conversations and much preferred the male companionship he found at his club or on the golf course.

In another short story written at about the same time for *Scribner's, The Lamp of Psyche,* Edith sounded a theme that

would recur again and again in her writing: a woman's disillusionment with the man she loves. After Delia's storybook
courtship and marriage to Laurence Corbett, an American living in Paris, the couple return home so she can introduce him
to her aunt, Mrs. Mason Hayne, a prominent Boston matriarch who had raised Delia as a child. At first, Mrs. Hayne
seems to share Delia's high opinion of Corbett, until one day
when the old woman asks her niece what service he had seen
during the Civil War. All of Mrs. Hayne's friends and relatives
had served gallantly during the war. Indeed, her own husband
had been killed at Bull Run. Delia has to admit that, as far as
she knows, Laurence never served at all.

Eventually, the couple return to Paris, but Delia continues
to be troubled by the fact that her husband had apparently
shirked his duty. One day, Laurence brings her a present, a
miniature of a young officer, and on the back is the inscription: "Fell at Chancellorsville, May 3, 1863." Finally, she cannot bear not knowing and asks him why he didn't serve:

> "Well—it all happened some time ago," he answered still
> smiling, "and the truth is that I've completely forgotten the
> excellent reasons that I doubtless had at the time for remain-
> ing at home."
>
> "Reasons for remaining at home? But there were none;
> every man of your age went to the war; no one stayed at home
> who wasn't lame, or blind, or deaf, or ill, or—" Her face
> blazed, her voice broke passionately.
>
> Corbett looked at her with rising amazement.
>
> "Or—" he said.
>
> "Or a coward," she flashed out. The miniature dropped
> from her hands, falling loudly on the polished floor.
>
> The two confronted each other in silence; Corbett was
> very pale.

"I've told you," he said at length. "That I was neither lame, deaf, blind, nor ill. Your classification is so simple that it will be easy for you to draw your own conclusion."

And very quietly, with that admirable air which always put him in the right, he walked out of the room.[2]

Later Delia would apologize to her husband. But nothing would ever be the same between them.

By the early 1890s, Edith had written several short stories for *Scribner's*, and her editor, Edward Burlingame, had even suggested that the firm might publish an entire book of her works. "I need hardly say how much I am flattered by Messrs. Scribner's proposition to publish my stories in a volume," she wrote him from Newport. "I have several more which you might not have seen."[3] But the volume was delayed because Burlingame rejected these later stories.

Writing from Florence in March 1894, Edith lamented:

I have just received your letter of March 13th, in which you tell me you don't like the story which I called "Something Exquisite." Pray, by the way, have no tender-hearted compunctions about criticizing my stories—Your criticism is most helpful to me, & I always recognize its justice. . . .

I should like to bring out the book without adding many more stories for I seem to have fallen into a period of groping, & perhaps, after publishing the volume, I might see better what direction I ought to take and acquire more assurance (the quality I feel I most lack). . . . I have lost confidence in myself at present. . .[4]

Indeed, Edith was losing complete sense of herself, and later that year she would suffer a nervous collapse that would continue for some time. Perhaps the breakdown was brought on by Edith's struggle to become a writer and the blow to her self-confidence when her stories were rejected. Or perhaps it was the growing realization that marriage to Teddy was sadly unfulfilling, and that constant travel could not compensate for her boredom or her sense of uselessness when she wasn't writing. We shall never know.

By 1896, Edith had recovered sufficiently to begin another writing project. Some years earlier she and Teddy had bought a new home in Newport, called Land's End. They hired Ogden Codman to redesign the interior, and out of this experience came a book, *The Decoration of Houses.* Under the joint authorship of Edith and Codman, it presented their ideas for a simpler type of interior design, in marked contrast with the style of late Victorian houses where rooms overflowed with all kinds of ostentatious furniture, paintings, artificial plants, and gaudy knickknacks. Although Edith considered herself a writer, she had to struggle to put her ideas on paper. Fortunately, her old friend Walter Berry, who had since become an international lawyer, visited Land's End that summer and came to her rescue:

> *I remember shyly asking him to look at my lumpy pages; and I remember his first shout of laughter (for he never flattered or pretended), and then his saying good naturedly: "Come, let's see what can be done," and settling down beside me to try to model the lump into a book.*[5]

Thus began a relationship that would continue throughout most of Edith's literary career. For Walter Berry served not only as her tireless editor and valued critic, but also her pri-

Edith Wharton during the early days of her marriage and on her way to establishing a writing career.

mary champion, encouraging Edith along the path of literary accomplishment. In several weeks, *The Decoration of Houses* was completed and Scribner's published it in 1897.

Meanwhile, Edith continued to produce short stories, including *The Pelican, The Muse's Tragedy,* and *Souls Belated,* which some critics believe to be one of her best. It describes Lydia Tillotson, a young woman who leaves her husband and runs away to Europe with another man, Ralph Gannett. The couple travel together until Lydia's divorce becomes final, then Ralph wants to marry her. But Lydia refuses, believing that marriage only prevents people from becoming close to each other:

"Do you know, I begin to see what marriage is for. It's to keep people away from each other. Sometimes I think that two people who love each other can be saved from madness only by the things that come between them—children, duties, visits, bores, relations—the things that protect married people from each other. We've been too close together—that has been our sin. We've seen the nakedness of each other's souls."[6]

Lydia recognizes that couples cannot deal with this "nakedness" and that the best they can hope for is a retreat into the separateness that marriage brings. Eventually she agrees to marry Ralph.

Edith's prodigious efforts finally gave her more than enough short stories for a book. With the help of Walter Berry, she selected the best of them, and in 1899 Scribner's published her first book of fiction, *The Greater Inclination*. In her autobiography, Edith wrote that "I had as yet no real personality of my own and was not to acquire one till my first volume of short stories was published. . . ."[7] It was an accomplishment that clearly left her feeling elated.

I had written short stories that were thought worthy of preservation! Was it the same insignificant I that I had always known? Any one walking along the streets might go into any bookshop, and say: "Please give me Edith Wharton's book," and the clerk, without bursting into incredulous laughter, would produce it, and be paid for it, and the purchaser would walk home with it and read it, and talk of it, and pass it on to other people to read! The whole business seemed too unreal to be anything but a practical joke played on me by some occult humorist; and my friends could not have been more astonished and incredulous than I was.[8]

The book received generally favorable reviews, but Edith was upset that Scribner's had not spent more money in advertising it. The same complaint would punctuate much of her correspondence with Scribner's during their long association.

--------------------------------- ❧ ---------------------------------

Although Edith had begun to receive the recognition she desired, it was already proving to be somewhat of a mixed blessing. New York's upper crust always considered writers unconventional and a woman writer far more unconventional than most. Instead of being praised for her literary accomplishments, Edith found herself the object of disapproval among the social elite that often distrusted intellectuals, especially if they were female. She was snubbed. Longing for a different environment, she persuaded Teddy to take her to London, but he quickly grew bored there, so they journeyed east to Switzerland and Italy. There she met an old acquaintance, French author Paul Bourget, and his wife, Minnie, who gave Edith some of the intellectual companionship she needed. Her travels through the magnificent countryside of the Italian Alps also became the subject of an article for *Scribner's* magazine. It was to be Edith's first travel article, but far from the last. Her wide-ranging skills would enable her to feel comfortable in a variety of genres.

As the new century began, Edith completed a novella that ran in installments in *Scribner's* magazine and was then published as her second book of fiction. In *The Touchstone,* Edith returned to her familiar theme of disillusionment in marriage. The hero, Stephen Glennard, finds the money he needs to marry a young woman by selling some intimate letters that had been written to him by a prominent fiction writer during their earlier love affair. At first Stephen's betrayal doesn't seem to bother his conscience, but eventually guilt gets the better of him and Glennard confesses to his wife that he has sold the letters. Although their marriage continues, her faith in him is severely shaken and can never be fully restored.

Once *The Touchstone* had been published, Edith and Teddy sailed for England, then traveled on to Italy for another vacation with the Bourgets. During these regular trips, she had been visiting historical sites and gathering material for a novel she hoped to write about Italian politics during the eighteenth century. In order to create an accurate picture of the period, Edith had also been reading extensively and even went so far as to borrow some books from the library of her old friend, Professor Charles Eliot Norton, one of Harvard University's most distinguished lecturers.

The Valley of Decision, like her earlier works, won high praise from reviewers when it was published in 1902. "It is a beautiful spectacle, that of our great country from Maine to California joining in a chorus of praise over the Valley!" she wrote Charles Eliot Norton's daughter, Sara.[9]

The successful publication of her books enabled Edith Wharton to finally throw off the image of herself as a plain, awkward woman out of step with the other females of her social circle. She had finally come into her own.

> *The reception of my books gave me the self-confidence I had so long lacked, and in the company of people who shared my tastes, and treated me as their equal, I ceased to suffer from the agonizing shyness which used to rob such encounters of all pleasure.*[10]

At the age of forty, Edith Wharton had emerged as one of America's leading fiction writers.

4

THE MOUNT

The Valley of Decision was the first book that Edith Wharton completed at The Mount, her new home in Lenox, Massachusetts. For several years Edith had been coming to Lenox during the summer, for she found the climate of the Berkshires much more pleasant than Newport. She had also grown bored with the people she met there. Newport had been transformed by wealthy New Yorkers, like the Astors and the Vanderbilts, from a vacation resort of modest houses to a showplace of huge mansions, monuments to crass materialism that Edith would later satirize in her novels.

Edith had named The Mount after the Long Island estate of her great grandfather, Ebenezer Stevens, but the house took its inspiration from an English country home that she had seen during one of her travels. Edith worked closely with the architect in drawing up the plans and with Teddy supervised construction. For a woman to play such a central role in these affairs was quite unusual for the period, but Edith had a keen eye for architecture and interior decoration, as she had already proven. What's more, it was her income, as well as Teddy's,

Edith and Teddy Wharton built a country house, The Mount, in Lenox,
Massachusetts.

that made The Mount affordable. Edith had been left money
from a variety of sources, including her father's estate; a relative, Joshua Jones; and by the death of her mother in 1901. As
a result, she had a sizable yearly income of about $22,000.[1]

Construction on The Mount began in 1901, and Edith
and Teddy moved into the house at the end of September
1902. It was the beginning of fall, one of the most beautiful
seasons in New England. And The Mount, which sat on a
small hill, had a magnificent view of the surrounding landscape
with its gold, bronze, and red colors. A cupola had been built
on top of the house from which guests could look out for
miles onto the magnificent Berkshire Hills. On the floor below
were the servants' bedrooms, for the Whartons had a full staff

to run the house—cook, maids, gardener, chauffeur—during the months that they were in residence and to maintain it while they traveled abroad. Edith, of course, supervised the staff (with Teddy's help) when she wasn't busy writing in her bedroom suite on the second floor, which also included Teddy's bedroom and bedrooms for guests. But the center of life at The Mount was the first floor and what lay beyond:

> *On the first floor there was a library, a drawing-room, and a dining-room with French doors opening on a broad terrace shaded by a great, striped awning. From this terrace the Whartons and their guests could survey the formal gardens laid out . . . like the Italian gardens she delighted in, and beyond this, lawn sloping to meadow up to the border of a pond framed with trees. On the other side of the house there was a kitchen-garden, a grape arbor, a small farm, and, surrounding the whole, a hundred-and-fifty acres of rolling woodland.*[2]

At The Mount, Edith gathered a circle of intellectual friends and created a social environment that enabled her to achieve what seemed impossible in Newport or New York: acceptance by her peers. She would often greet guests at the door, carrying a small dog under her arm, for "it was a fact that dogs—small dogs and preferably Pekinese—were among the main joys of her being, and had been since she was a child."[3] Edith would write each morning with a dog by her side, and she and Teddy were frequently photographed with one or more of these small animals in their laps, on their shoulders, or in their arms.

Once inside this "salon of the Berkshires," a visitor could expect the conversation to range from literature and art to Italian villas and English gardens. Edith's infectious laughter would fill the drawing room, as she was frequently the only woman present. Her guests might include Walter Berry; Bay Lodge, a poet and the son of Senator Henry Cabot Lodge from Massachusetts; the author Brooks Adams, whose illustrious ancestors had been American presidents; Gaillard Lapsley, an American who taught history at Cambridge University in England; Edith's old friend Egerton Winthrop; novelist Robert Grant; Edward Robinson, director of New York's Metropolitan Museum of Art; and the man with whom she developed one of her closest friendships, Henry James.

Almost twenty years older than Edith, Henry James had been born in Washington Square, a mile south of the brownstone where she grew up. Like the Joneses, the James family had also lived in Newport and Europe. After attending Harvard Law School and writing for the *Atlantic Monthly,* Henry James had eventually decided to make his permanent home in England. From there he wrote *The American, Daisy Miller,* and *The Portrait of a Lady*—novels that made him world famous.

As a younger woman, Edith had been awed by James. In her autobiography, she described her first encounter with him during the 1880s at the home of a mutual friend in Paris. Edith had worn her most attractive dress in order to catch his attention, for she felt very insignificant in James's presence. "But, alas, it neither gave me the courage to speak, nor attracted the attention of the great man. The evening was a failure, and I went humbled and discouraged."[4] Her second encounter with James occurred a year or two later in Venice. This time she wore a beautiful hat to attract his notice, but the result was exactly the same.

In 1899, following the publication of *The Greater Inclina-*

It was the American writer Henry James who encouraged Edith Wharton to write about New York. They became close friends.

tion, the Whartons visited England. Edith craved the company of literary people with whom she might achieve a feeling of acceptance, which seemed so sorely lacking in New York. Edith and Teddy attended a round of dinners and receptions in London where she met the historian George Trevelyan, the novelist Thomas Hardy, and several women writers who, she was heartened to discover, were revered by English society. Then they traveled into the country to a house party where she encountered the artist John Singer Sargent and once again saw Henry James. But again nothing came of it.

A year later, Edith sent James a copy of one of her short stories, and he wrote back a mixed review, containing praise as well as criticism. Although James was very favorably impressed with Edith's first novel, *The Valley of Decision,* he also advised her to concentrate on what she knew best—"the American subject." "Do New York!" he exhorted her.[5]

Although Teddy never enjoyed England, Edith kept returning year after year, feeling even more at home there than she sometimes did in America. As she once wrote Sara Norton:

> *My first few weeks in America are always miserable, because the tastes I am cursed with are all of a kind that cannot be gratified here. . . . I feel in America as you say you do in England—out of sympathy with everything. And in England I like it all—institutions, traditions, mannerisms, conservatisms, everything but the women's clothes, & the having to go to church every Sunday.*[6]

In early 1904, Edith and Teddy stopped in London, and Henry James came up from Lamb House, his home in Rye, to visit. Later the Whartons traveled across the channel, bought a new car in France, and motored south to the coast where their itinerary took them to Cannes and Monte Carlo. Although automobile travel was relatively new at this time, and very unreliable, the Whartons embraced it wholeheartedly. Henry James loved motoring too, but he never did learn to drive and often relied on the Whartons to take him with them. In fact, when they returned to England from France later in 1904, they journeyed down to Rye and carried James off for a ride in their car.

For Edith, the trips up the winding, cobbled road to Lamb House and the hours spent together with James were among the most memorable of her life, and she recalled him lovingly in her autobiography:

> *There he stood on the doorstep, the white paneled hall with its old prints and crowded bookcases forming a background to*

his heavy loosely clothed figure. Arms outstretched, lips and eyes twinkling, he came down to the car, uttering cries of mock amazement and mock humility at the undeserved honor of my visit. . . . Then, arm in arm, through the oak-paneled morning-room we wandered out onto the thin worn turf of the garden, with its ancient mulberry tree, its unkempt flower borders . . . and the scent of roses spiced with a strong smell of the sea.[7]

Sometimes Edith would stay for extended periods at Lamb House. Both she and James would spend the mornings writing—he pacing up and down his garden room dictating to a secretary, while she wrote in another part of the house. Then they would walk into town for lunch, which was often followed by a motor trip into the countryside. One afternoon, they drove to Bodiam Castle, which had been built in the fourteenth century to ward off attacks from the French. Now a crumbling fortress, it was flanked by four huge stone towers and surrounded by a large moat. As James looked across at the battlements, he sighed: "Summer afternoon—summer afternoon; to me those have always been the two most beautiful words in the English language."[8]

Describing the warm friendship that gradually developed between herself and James, Edith wrote:

Perhaps it was our common sense of fun that first brought about our understanding. The real marriage of true minds is for any two people to possess a sense of humour or irony pitched in exactly the same key, so that their joint glances at any subject cross like interarching searchlights.[9]

James often referred to Edith as the "pendulum woman" because of her frequent trips back and forth across the Atlantic. But in 1904, James himself came home to America for a speaking tour, and in October he stayed at The Mount. And of course, there were motor trips through the beautiful Berkshire countryside. And, although the posted speed limit was only twenty miles per hour, that didn't prevent James and Edith from traveling as far west as the Hudson River or visiting the home of Charles Eliot Norton, who was not only Edith's friend but James's, too, in Ashfield, Massachusetts.

During her lifetime, Edith's fiction was often compared with the novels of Henry James, because their writing style and their subjects often seemed similar—at least to certain reviewers. It was a comparison, however, that Edith disliked and promptly rejected. In a letter to her editor, William Crary Brownell, regarding the reviews of a new collection of short stories published in 1904, she wrote:

> *I return the reviews with many thanks. I have never before been discouraged by criticism, because when the critics have found fault with me I have usually abounded in their sense, & seen, as I thought, a way of doing better the next time; but the continued cry that I am an echo of Mr. James (whose books of the last ten years I can't read, much as I delight in the man) & the assumption that the people I write about are not "real" . . . makes me feel rather hopeless.*[10]

This new collection, in fact, contains stories that modern critics consider among Edith's finest. In *The Other Two,* for example, the subject is marriage and divorce. While still considered somewhat scandalous around the turn of the century, the divorce rate had been increasing in the United States and would actually jump fifteenfold between 1870 and 1920.

Edith's story gives the subject a humorous turn as she describes the predicament of Waythorn, a successful businessman, whose wife has taken him as her third husband. Although Waythorn is at first comfortable with his marriage, disillusionment eventually sets in. His wife's first husband, Haskett, begins appearing regularly to visit the couple's child, whom Waythorn has graciously taken into his home. Gradually, he develops a grudging respect for Haskett who is trying to maintain a close relationship with his daughter, and Waythorn wonders whether Alice—his wife—may have been partly responsible for the couple's divorce. Then he is forced to transact a business deal with Alice's second husband, Varick. Surprisingly, Waythorn finds that he enjoys working with the man, and they continue to bump into each other at social occasions around New York City. One evening, however, he chances upon his wife talking to Varick and this distresses him:

> She was "as easy as an old shoe"—a shoe that too many feet had worn. Her elasticity was the result of tension in too many different directions. Alice Haskett—Alice Varick—Alice Waythorn—she had been each in turn and had left hanging to each name a little of her privacy, a little of her personality, a little of the inmost self where the unknown god abides.[11]

Edith Wharton did not end the story, however, with Waythorn's disillusionment. Eventually he begins to appreciate his wife's remarkable ability at attracting and even satisfying not only himself, but his two predecessors as well. Then one afternoon, Waythorn returns home to find Haskett there again, and while the two men are talking, Varick arrives breathlessly to discuss an important business deal. To complete this unusual scene, Alice unexpectedly returns home from a shopping trip, enters the drawing room and, without missing a beat, begins serving tea to her three gentlemen.

In one of Edith's most humorous short stories, *Expiation,* she introduces us to a society matron named Mrs. Fetherel, who has written a juicy novel titled *Fast and Loose.* This was, in fact, the title of a novella that Edith had written in the late 1870s but never published. Although Mrs. Fetherel compares herself with Tolstoy and Ibsen, daring "to show up the hollowness of social conventions"[12] and expose the scandalous behavior of New York society, she vehemently protests to her dear friend Mrs. Clinch that she has not written the book to be a best-seller. "Mrs. Clinch was unperturbed. 'Perhaps that's just as well,' she returned, with a philosophic shrug. 'The surprise will be all the pleasanter, I mean. For of course it's going to sell tremendously; especially if you can get the press to denounce it.' "[13]

Unfortunately, the press doesn't cooperate. The reviewers dub the novel a "harmless story," and it languishes on the shelves of the bookstores—until divine fate suddenly intervenes. It arrives in the form of Mrs. Fetherel's uncle, the Bishop of Ossining, himself a writer of third-rate morality stories.

While sitting in his niece's drawing room, the bishop laments that if the critics would only denounce one of his books as scandalous it would become an instant best-seller, and he could use the royalties to decorate his church. When Mrs. Fetherel relates this conversation to Mrs. Clinch, she immediately suggests that the bishop decry *Fast and Loose* from the pulpit. At first, Mrs. Fetherel is skeptical:

"I suppose every book must stand or fall on its own merits,"
she said in an unconvinced tone.

"Bosh! That view is as extinct as the post chaise and the packet ship—it belongs to the time when people read books. Nobody does that now. . . . "[14]

Eventually, Mrs. Fetherel decides to follow her friend's advice, and *Fast and Loose* becomes an overnight success. It's a story that seems equally as appropriate today as it did when Edith Wharton wrote it almost a century ago.

5

THE HOUSE OF MIRTH

W hen Henry James urged Edith Wharton to "Do New York," he could not have known that she would do exactly that in her next novel. Edith began working on *The House of Mirth* in the summer of 1903, but over the next year the project moved along very slowly. She seemed easily distracted by a busy social schedule at The Mount, her regular trips to Europe with Teddy, and her efforts to complete a series of articles on the Italian villas located around Rome and northward, which would later be published as a book. Then Edward Burlingame of *Scribner's* magazine asked Edith if she could complete *The House of Mirth* ahead of schedule, so the magazine could begin serialization in early 1905 to replace another novel that had failed to meet its deadline. Suddenly, she found herself under enormous pressure.

I have always been a slow worker and was then a very inexperienced one, and I was to be put to the severest test that a novelist can be subjected: My novel was to be exposed to public comment before I had worked it out to its climax. What

that climax was to be I had known before I began. My last
page is always latent in my first; but the intervening windings
of the way become clear only as I write, and now I was asked
to gallop over them before I had even traced them out![1]

Nevertheless, the demands of finishing the story so quickly
profoundly shaped Edith's development as a writer. "Not only
did it give me what I most lacked—self-confidence—but it
bent me to the discipline of the daily task. . . ." And with
somewhat false modesty, she added: "It was good to be turned
from a drifting amateur into a professional. . . ."[2]

Edith successfully met Burlingame's schedule for serialization in *Scribner's* magazine, and in the fall of 1905 Scribner's
published *The House of Mirth* in book form. Demand for it was
so great that from an original edition of only 30,000 copies,
the novel repeatedly went back to press until 140,000 were in
print by the end of the year. By early 1906, *The House of Mirth*
had become America's best-selling novel and the most successful book Scribner's had ever published. Readers from across
the country sent Edith hundreds of letters praising the book.

In *The House of Mirth*, Edith Wharton presents her most
engaging heroine—Lily Bart. We meet Lily at the opening of
the story in a bustling crowd at New York's Grand Central
Station as she is seen through the eyes of Lawrence Selden, a
modestly successful lawyer whose on-again, off-again love
affair with her will form a central theme of the book. Selden is
at once admiring and distinctly critical of the beautiful Miss
Bart. "Everything about her was at once vigorous and
exquisite, at once strong and fine. He had a confused sense that
she must have cost a great deal to make, that a great many dull
and ugly people must, in some mysterious way, have been sacrificed to produce her."[3]

After walking along Madison Avenue, Lily and Selden eventually find themselves standing in front of his apartment building, and although it is considered almost indecent for an unmarried woman to accompany a man to his flat unchaperoned, Lily impulsively agrees to accept Selden's invitation for tea. Lily's impulsive nature is one of her most endearing qualities, but it consistently seems to land her in trouble, and this occasion is no exception. As she emerges from Selden's building, she runs into an old acquaintance, Simon Rosedale, and after lying unconvincingly about her reasons for being in the neighborhood, she hurries back to Grand Central Station in time to catch a train to the country.

Lily's destination is Bellomont, the palatial estate of Gus and Judy Trenor, where she has been invited for yet another house party, part of the continuous round of social engagements that comprise the fabric of her life. Since Lily has only a small income and is totally untrained for any kind of work, she must live off her wealthy friends, at least until she succeeds in capturing a rich husband. But for Miss Bart time is beginning to run out, as she matter-of-factly confides to Selden:

> "I've been about too long—people are getting tired of me; they are beginning to say I ought to marry. . . ."
>
> "Isn't marriage your vocation? Isn't it what you're all brought up for?"
>
> . . . She shook her head wearily. "I threw away one or two good chances when I first came out—I suppose every girl does; and you know I am horribly poor, and very expensive. I must have a great deal of money."[4]

At Bellomont, the current object of Lily's attentions is Percy Gryce, the doltish heir to a huge family fortune, whose primary interest is his expensive collection of dusty Americana.

Lily easily charms Gryce with her considerable feminine wiles, and he seems poised to propose marriage. But Lily can only imagine how boring life will become once she is married to Gryce. On Sunday morning when Gryce is expecting Lily to accompany him to church, she intentionally misses the carriage that will take them to the service, preferring to spend the day with Selden who has arrived late at Bellomont. Edith Wharton describes Lily's conflicted mind as she chooses Selden's company instead of pursuing her own financial security: "There was in her at the moment two beings, one drawing deep breaths of freedom and exhilaration, the other gasping for air in a little black prison-house of fears."[5] This prison image will recur throughout the novel.

As they bask in the sunny glow of a warm afternoon, Lily and Selden define their ideas of success. For Selden, it is "personal freedom," what he calls a "kind of republic of the spirit" that enables him to remain aloof from a tawdry interest in money and social climbing that seems to concern most of the other people around him.[6] Edith Wharton created Selden from some of the men who formed her own circle of friends— sensitive intellectuals who talked about life without ever really engaging in it. They lacked strength, and Edith knew that. Selden's "republic of the spirit" is a mere rationalization; he is able to rub shoulders with New York's social elite without ever feeling that any of their crass values have rubbed off on him. He remains the constant observer, refusing to become involved with anyone of his set, including Lily, no matter how strongly he is attracted to her. Similarly, Lily constantly reminds herself that she cannot become involved with Selden because he does not possess the necessary amount of money.

Meanwhile, Lily's quarry has slipped away. Percy Gryce is scared off by Bertha Dorset, a female barracuda who darts from one adulterous relationship to the next (including a recent affair with Selden) and who envies Lily for her beauty and the attentions that men pay to her. Consequently, Lily returns to New York City to live with her wealthy aunt, Mrs. Peniston.

Edith Wharton had a keen eye for satire, and she possessed the ability to sum up a character with a few satirical strokes of her pen. Mrs. Peniston is no exception:

> She belonged to the class of old New Yorkers who have always lived well, dressed expensively, and done little else; and to these inherited obligations Mrs. Peniston faithfully conformed. She had always been a looker-on at life, and her mind resembled one of those little mirrors which her Dutch ancestors were accustomed to affix to their upper windows so that from the depths of an impenetrable domesticity they might see what was happening in the street.[7]

With another quick thrust, Edith also deflates Lily's cousin, Grace Stepney, whose "mind was like a kind of moral fly-paper, to which the buzzing items of gossip were drawn by a fatal attraction, and where they hung fast in the toils of an inexorable memory."[8] When Grace happens on a few choice tidbits about Lily, whom she envies, she immediately passes them on to Mrs. Peniston. Apparently, Lily had lost heavily betting at bridge during her stay at Bellomont and had asked Gus Trenor if he might help her recoup her losses. Lily naively believes that Gus will invest a portion of her meager income in the stock market and make "a killing." Of course, Gus imagines that Lily knows it is his own money he is risking, and when his investments begin to yield rich dividends, he expects something from her in return. Luring Lily to his townhouse on the pretext that his wife wants to see her, Trenor drunkenly confronts Lily in his drawing room. But she pushes him away

The wealthy families of old New York satirized by Edith Wharton lived in splendid homes designed by the leading architects of the day. These buildings, like the one designed by Richard Morris Hunt, shown here, transformed New York City.

just as she had done repeatedly before and races from the house.

Throughout the novel, Edith Wharton continually examines the influence of money, for many of her characters had, as she said, come into "sudden possession" of it "without inherited obligations."[9] She meant *The House of Mirth* to be an accurate reflection of New York City, which was being transformed by the nouveaux riches. People like the Vanderbilts, the Havemeyers, and the Goulds were no different than the Trenors or the Rosedales, who expected their money could be used to buy anything, including social position and other people.

At a fashionable party, for example, Rosedale sees Lily appear in a tableau—wearing the costume of a woman in a famous painting by the artist Joshua Reynolds. He is so awe-struck by her beauty that he wants to have her portrait painted, believing it will appreciate 100 percent in ten years. Later, he proposes to Lily, believing that she can help him achieve the social position he so desperately craves. "I've got the money . . . and what I want is the woman—and I mean to have her too."[10]

Rosedale regards Lily as an object that can be bought, just as Trenor does, but she refuses him too. The only one who sees her differently is Selden, but he is far too detached and far too critical of Lily to ever really help her.

Escaping from her problems in New York, Lily accepts an invitation aboard the Dorsets' yacht, which is cruising along the Riviera. Bertha Dorset wants Lily there to keep her husband occupied while she pursues yet another illicit relationship. And Lily willingly obliges, for she is prepared to pay the necessary price to sit at society's banquet table. Meanwhile, Lily has received an offer of marriage from an Italian prince who had met her in Cannes, but before he can finalize the details, she begins a flirtation with his stepson that puts an immediate end to the marriage plans. Carry Fisher, a divorcée and a friend of Lily's, sees her perhaps more clearly than anyone else in the novel. As she tells Selden:

"That's Lily all over, you know: she works like a slave preparing the ground and sowing her seeds, but the day she ought to be reaping the harvest, she oversleeps or goes off on a picnic. . . . Sometimes . . . I think it's just flightiness, and sometimes I think it's because, at heart, she despises the things she's trying for. And it's the difficulty of deciding that makes her such an interesting study."[11]

None of the other characters seems to have this problem, not Trenor or Rosedale, and certainly not Bertha Dorset. For when Bertha's affair is about to be discovered by her husband, she accuses Lily of having a liaison with him and banishes her from the yacht. Lily must return to New York in disgrace, where she finds that her aunt has died, leaving her almost nothing and bequeathing the estate instead to Grace Stepney. Without the prospects of any money, Lily finds herself almost completely abandoned by New York society, which values wealth above all else.

Throughout the novel Lily has been caught in a downward spiral—as she is rejected by her suitors, falls prey to Bertha Dorset, and is finally cut out of her aunt's will.

For the moment, at least, Lily is rescued by Carry Fisher. Carry survives by using her contacts to help the nouveaux riches break into society. And she introduces Lily to the rich Samuel Gormers, explaining that Lily is someone who can help them arrange fashionable parties and contribute to the general amusement of their friends. Although Lily is fully prepared to pay this price to maintain a fashionable lifestyle, she also recognizes that in entering the Gormers' set she has descended a rung on the social scale. And her stop there is destined to be short-lived, for once again Bertha Dorset appears to spread rumors about Lily, and she must flee.

Ironically, Lily has all along held the means to reverse her fortunes—a group of love letters have come into her possession, which were written by Bertha Dorset to Lawrence Selden. If these were to fall into the wrong hands, they could destroy Bertha's position. Simon Rosedale and Carry Fisher—both hard-headed realists who are also aware that these letters exist—urge Lily to use them against Bertha. As Rosedale bluntly tells her: "Everybody knows what Mrs. Dorset is, and her best friends wouldn't believe her on oath where their own interests were concerned; but as long as they're out of the row, it's much easier to follow her lead than to set themselves against it, and you've simply been sacrificed to their laziness and selfishness."[12]

Indeed, this was the central theme, as well as the central problem, that Edith Wharton dealt with in writing her novel. How could she give "a society of irresponsible pleasure-seekers" (her *House of Mirth*) some greater significance? Wharton replied: "The answer was that a frivolous society can acquire dramatic significance only through what its frivolity destroys. Its tragic implication lies in its power of debasing people and ideals. The answer, in short, was my heroine, Lily Bart."[13] No doubt there were many Lily Barts in nineteenth century America—genteel women with meager financial resources who had been trained to do little else but "adorn and delight" and eventually become someone's wife. They were prisoners of a rigid social system. As Lily, herself, frankly puts it: ". . . I am a very useless person. I can hardly be said to have an independent existence. I was just a screw or a cog in the great machine I called life, and when I dropped out of it I found I was of no use anywhere else."[14]

As long as Lily refuses to use the letters, her fate appears sealed. For a time she works as a secretary to a well-to-do divorcée from the West who comes to New York hoping to marry one of the local blue bloods. But once again Lily realizes that she has dropped another rung in the social scale, and just as before, she is forced to leave her position under pressure from her former friends in high society.

As a final desperate measure, Lily tries to support herself by working in a local millinery shop, but she proves completely unsuited to this kind of drudgery. It is only then, at the eleventh hour, that she decides to confront Bertha Dorset with the letters. But on her way to the Dorsets' town house, Lily

decides to stop at Selden's apartment. She is so moved by being
in his presence that she rashly throws the letters into the fire:

> ". . . you gave me the chance to escape from my life, and I
> refused it: refused it because I was a coward. Afterward I saw
> my mistake: I saw I could never be happy with what had con-
> tented me before. But it was too late: you had judged me—I
> understood. It was too late for happiness but not too late to be
> helped by the thought of what I had missed."[15]

Unfortunately, Lily attributes far more moral strength to
Selden than he actually possesses. She allows herself to be
judged by his principles—principles that he is incapable of following, as his affair with Bertha Dorset shows only too clearly.
Lily is the one with the moral courage. And even with all her
indecision and impulsiveness, her naivete and her seeming
shallowness, Lily possesses a flesh-and-blood humanness that is
far beyond the reach of the bloodless Selden. In those last
tragic moments of the novel, when she takes the overdose of
sleeping potion that ends her life, Lily Bart slips out of his
reach forever.

6

TEDDY WHARTON AND MORTON FULLERTON

Over the next several years, following the success of *The House of Mirth,* Edith established herself in London and, more permanently, in Paris. For while Edith loved England and her visits with close friend Henry James, it was Paris that she gradually adopted as her second home. After the publication of *The House of Mirth,* her old friend Paul Bourget, who had also become an acclaimed author, introduced Edith to the exclusive Parisian salon society. At these salons—house gatherings often hosted by a member of the French nobility—artists, playwrights, poets, politicians, and members of the diplomatic corps would regularly dine together and enjoy conversation. Edith found all of this most stimulating. She was a frequent guest, for example, at the salon of Comtesse Anna de Noailles, a poet and novelist, who frequently conducted her salon from the comfort of her chaise lounge.

Edith returned to Paris every year and in 1907 rented an apartment at 58 Rue de Varenne, a quiet, tree-lined street in the exclusive Faubourg St. Germain section of the city. There she established her own salon. In time, Edith created the same type of intimate intellectual circle she had developed at The Mount. At the same time, she continued to write keenly about the upper classes—their foibles and values. In short stories such as *The Last Asset* and novellas like *Madame de Treymes,* Edith examined the clash of cultures, as Americans and French aristocrats tried to understand each other's conflicting attitudes about marriage and divorce.

While Edith was absorbed in these projects, the familiar routines of her own life began to break down, and she became like the traveler who is driving down an unfamiliar road without a road map. Her marriage to Teddy, which had always bumped along somehow, now began to come apart. Meanwhile, at the age of forty-five, Edith fell deeply in love, possibly for the first time. His name was Morton Fullerton.

Who can tell how early in their marriage boredom set in for the Whartons. At first, they must have seemed like most other couples of the wealthy upper classes, content to idle away their lives traveling between America and Europe, attending formal dinners, dancing at gala balls, and spending lots of money. The Whartons were childless and lacked that anchor in their relationship. Instead, they lavished their attentions on small dogs, which appear in so many of their photographs—sometimes two or three of them, sitting on Edith's shoulders or in Teddy's lap like small children. In other photographs, the Whartons are seated in their car, which symbolized a life that was constantly on the move. Even Henry James, who usually enjoyed motoring with the Whartons, sometimes had to admit that he found their pace exhausting. James, who lived frugally and constantly worried about money, also disapproved of the Whartons' lavish lifestyle—with a magnificent home in the Berkshires, a spacious apartment in an expensive section of Paris, and a staff of servants at their beck and call. What James must have realized, however, is that the Whartons

Teddy Wharton at the time of his marriage to Edith.

desperately needed material pleasures to make up for the pleasure that was so obviously missing in their relationship, just as they needed to maintain their hectic pace because it left them with very little time to confront the fact that they were really not meant to live together.

Teddy Wharton was an easygoing man of leisure, like so many of the characters who appear in Edith's novels. He had no ambition. His few interests were those he could pursue outdoors—hunting, fishing, and motoring—and he seemed content with the male companionship that his club provided—

typical of most other men of his class and generation. But
Edith was hardly the typical wife—someone who stayed at
home, raised her children, and presided at lavish social occasions. She needed to breathe an entirely different atmo-
sphere—one that was filled with poets and artists, playwrights,
and novelists. And she was determined to be accepted as their
equal. Since Teddy seemed uncomfortable with Edith's ambi-
tions, as well as many of her friends, the Whartons spent more
and more time apart. Edith, for example, often visited her
friends' homes on her own. As her literary success grew, she
began to overwhelm Teddy, with disastrous consequences for
their marriage.

Serious cracks in the Whartons' relationship had already
begun to show in 1902. During the year that Edith published
her first novel, *The Valley of Decision,* and critics hailed her as
one of America's leading fiction writers, Teddy suffered a nervous collapse. Although the Whartons may not have recognized the connection, Edith's fame had probably made Teddy
insecure. He recovered, but only to suffer a relapse in the summer of 1902 and again in 1903. Although Edith disliked Newport, she agreed to a short vacation there for Teddy's sake. But
after returning to The Mount, he began to suffer again, so she
took him back to Newport. In early 1904, Teddy seemed well
enough to travel to Europe, and for the next several years there
were no relapses.

But Teddy's recovery proved only temporary. After leaving
The Mount and sailing to Paris at the end of 1907, he experienced another breakdown. As Edith Wharton's biographer
R.W.B. Lewis explains: ". . . the environment she was building
about her in Paris was suffocating to the easygoing lover of
fishing. . . . Teddy was stifled by the salons of Paris and the
French literary acclaim of his wife . . . not to mention his total
financial dependence upon her. . . ."[1]

Although Teddy received some income from his family, it

in no way matched the sum Edith had inherited from her parents, combined with the royalties she had begun to earn from the sale of her books. As Edith's fame and fortune rose, Teddy's health steadily declined. Writing from Paris in March 1908, Edith told Charles Eliot Norton that although Teddy's nervous collapse had ended, "his troublesome gout still persists, & the Dr. thinks that only baths will really cure it . . . There is no good cure here to which one can go at this season, & he thinks of sailing a few weeks before me, & taking the baths at the Hot Springs [a famous spa in Arkansas] early in April, as he is most anxious not to be laid up this summer."[2]

There is ample evidence that the Whartons' relationship, which had not been close for many years, was now being pushed to the breaking point, as Edith was forced to cope with Teddy's illnesses. At The Mount, during the summer, he suffered another collapse, which continued after their return to Paris that winter, along with a flair up of his gout. "He's the worst patient I've ever seen," she wrote Sara Norton. Teddy went south to the French coast where it was hoped the milder weather might help him recover. But as Edith admitted to Sara: "It is very wearing, and I am utterly tired."[3] Eventually they returned to Paris, where Teddy received further treatment. But none of the doctors seemed able to satisfy him, and he finally sailed for home to America, while Edith remained behind in Paris.

Henry James, who knew about the long ordeal Edith had endured that winter, tried to give her the best advice he could under the circumstances: "Sit loose and live in the day—don't borrow trouble, and remember that nothing happens as we forecast it—but always with interesting and, as it were, refreshing differences."[4]

———————————— ❧ ————————————

James may not have realized just how appropriate his

advice seemed to Edith at the time. For her life had already taken a turn that she could never have forecast—and one that made the prospect of her continued marriage to Teddy all the more difficult to bear. She had fallen in love.

Morton Fullerton was an American, a graduate of Harvard and a friend of the Nortons and Henry James. For many years he had written for the *London Times,* covering events in Paris. He had met Edith there in 1907, when he was forty-one, visited her at The Mount that summer and seemed easily drawn into her select circle of male friends. But it soon became clear that Morton Fullerton meant far more to Edith than the other single men she had drawn around her. In March, as Teddy prepared to leave for Hot Springs, she wrote Fullerton:"Dear . . . if you can't come into the room without my feeling all over me a ripple of flame, & if, wherever you touch me, a heart beats under your touch, & if, when you hold me, & I don't speak, it's because all the words in me seem to have become throbbing pulses, & all my thoughts are a great golden blur."[5] After Teddy had departed, Edith and Fullerton spent many hours together sharing their private thoughts, as they strolled along the tree-lined streets of Paris, visited galleries or dined at out-of-the-way restaurants. He was a guest at Edith's salon where she entertained the American writer Henry Adams, her publisher Charles Scribner, and her old friend Egerton Winthrop. That spring when he came to Paris, Henry James accompanied Edith and Fullerton on an automobile trip.

As Edith well knew, this was not Morton Fullerton's first romantic involvement, and she was afraid lest she demand too much of their relationship . . . afraid that he might find her tiresome. At other times, however, Edith's hesitations were completely overcome by her emotions. Writing to Fullerton just before she set sail for America in the spring of 1908, Edith left no doubt about the role he now played in her life:

*I am mad about you Dear Heart and sick at the thought of
our parting and the days of separation and longing that are
to follow. It is a wonderful world that you have created for me
. . . but how I am to adjust it to the other world is difficult
to conceive. Perhaps when I am once more on land my mental
vision may be clearer—at present, in the whole universe I see
but one thing, am conscious of but one thing, you, and our
love for each other.*[6]

After she returned to The Mount, Fullerton's letters reached
her regularly. Then, without warning the letters stopped, and
Edith fell into despair. At last, Fullerton wrote her again, but
this interlude was followed by more silence. Edith could not
believe that Fullerton was so fickle in his affection. "Dear,
won't you tell me soon the meaning of this silence? . . . I re-
read your letters the other day, & I will not believe that the
man who wrote them did not feel them. . . ."[7]

Gradually, her feelings for Fullerton began to cool. Her
longtime friend Charles Eliot Norton was dying, and Edith
tried to lend as much support as she could to his daughter,
Sara, during her terrible ordeal. Returning to Europe at the
end of the year, she wrote Fullerton stiffly from London, asking that he return all her notes and letters. After Teddy arrived
in Paris, suffering more than ever, Edith headed to the south
of France to help him recover.

By the springtime, however, with Teddy back in America,
Edith and Fullerton had once again resumed their relationship. In
June, they traveled to London together and dined with Henry
James. As she wrote Fullerton in late summer: "Before . . . I had
no personal life: Since then you have given me all imaginable
joy." But Edith had also come to understand the changeable
nature of Fullerton's feelings, and in the same letter she also told
him: "It is impossible . . . that our lives should run parallel much

longer. . . . I know how unequal the exchange is between us, how little I have to give that a man like you can care for, & how ready I am, when the transition comes, to be again the good comrade you once found me."[8]

The transition that Edith talked about was pushed along when Teddy returned from America late that fall, and she had to deal with some new problems. First, he announced that he had become involved with another woman. What's more, he had also taken money from Edith's accounts to spend on that woman. Once this was finally cleared up and Teddy had returned the money, it was still obvious that his emotional condition had not improved. However, Edith still felt responsible for helping him find relief. After consulting various specialists and considering several alternative cures, Teddy finally agreed to enter a Swiss sanitorium in 1910. By this time Edith admitted to Fullerton that she was thoroughly exhausted—not only from caring for Teddy but also from putting up with the advice she had received from his family:

> The Whartons . . . refuse to recognize the strain I am under, & the impossibility, for a person with nerves strung like mine, to go on leading the life I am now leading. . . . If I try to escape, he will follow; if I protest, & say I want to be left alone, they will say that I deserted him when he was ill. . . . What, in these conditions, do you advise?[9]

For the present, at least, Edith decided to stay with Teddy. Before the end of the year he had not only left the sanitorium but departed on a trip around the world with one of his close friends. Edith remained behind, but not to continue the relationship with Morton Fullerton. As far as he was concerned it

had already lasted long enough, and Edith recognized that he
wanted his freedom:

   "You are as free as you were before we ever met," she
wrote him in June 1910. "If you ever doubted this, doubt it no
more."[10]

7

ETHAN FROME

Although Edith's personal life may have been in tremendous turmoil, she still continued to write and publish regularly between 1906 and 1911. Writing provided a safe harbor for Edith and gave her a feeling of control when all else seemed to be falling apart around her. It also reaffirmed her sense of identity and gave her real accomplishments at a time when she sorely needed them.

Very little escaped Edith's discerning eye or her skillful, versatile pen. Her trips across France with Henry James during these years became travel articles for the *Atlantic Monthly,* and later they were gathered together with others in a book, *A Motor Flight Through France,* that was published in 1908.

In the tradition of Edgar Allen Poe, Edith had also become an accomplished spinner of ghost stories, and Scribner's published a collection, *Tales of Men and Ghosts,* in 1910. One of these tales, *The Eyes,* which critics call among her best, describes a writer who is haunted by a terrible pair of accusing eyes that appear at his bed in the dark of night.

Edith's best known work from this period, indeed the one

for which she is still best remembered, is a small masterpiece, *Ethan Frome*. The novella began as a language exercise. When Edith decided to live in Paris part of the year, she wanted to improve her conversational French and hired a tutor. As one of her practice exercises, she began writing the story of Ethan Frome in French some time during 1907. Before it was finished, Edith put the story away for several years, then resumed it.

From her home at The Mount, Edith had traveled along the byways of New England and observed the harsh, barren existence of many of its inhabitants. While previous writers had sought to romanticize life on a New England farm, Edith presented what to her was a far more realistic picture, complete with all its starkness and desolation. But far from a depressing experience, writing the novella was for her a labor of love:

> *For years I had wanted to draw life as it really was in the derelict mountain villages of New England, a life even in my time, and a thousandfold more a generation earlier, utterly unlike that seen through the rose-colored spectacles of my pre-decessors. . . . In those days the snow-bound villages of Western Massachusetts were still grim places . . . slow mental and moral starvation were hidden away behind the paintless wooden house-fronts of the long village street or in the isolated farm-houses on the neighboring hills. . . .*[1]

The plot of *Ethan Frome* is very simple: Called home from his studies at an engineering institute because of his father's death, Ethan must take over the running of the poor family farm and scratch out a living from the barren soil. Eventually, his mother also falls ill, and a relative named Zeena comes to care for her. After his mother's death, Ethan cannot bear the thought of living alone so he asks Zeena, who is several years older, to marry him. Gradually she too falls prey to her own real and imagined illnesses, and her cousin, Mattie Silver, is summoned to help run the household. Mattie and Ethan fall passionately in love, but their affair is doomed. In a final desperate act, the lovers decide to commit suicide by hurtling down a steep snow-covered hill and running their sled into a huge elm tree. However, the suicide is a failure. Instead, Ethan is grotesquely maimed and Mattie becomes an invalid, cared for by a newly revitalized Zeena, who has suddenly found new meaning for her life.

Critics have seen in *Ethan Frome* the story of Edith's own marriage. Like Ethan, she was shackled to a long-suffering, chronically ill spouse and longed for relief in a relationship with someone else. Even the names of the characters seem to reflect Edith's own experience—Ethan and Edith, Mattie and Morton Fullerton.

Set in Starkfield, Massachusetts—even the name suggests utter desolation—most of the story is told as a flashback, a chronicle of the events that led up to Ethan's horrible injury twenty years earlier. The book begins by introducing us to a middle-aged Ethan, much as Edith had introduced us to Lily Bart at the beginning of *The House of Mirth*. But what a difference! Ethan is described as "stiffened and grizzled" with "something bleak and unapproachable in his face," and with "the careless powerful look he had, in spite of a lameness checking each step like the jerk of a chain."[2] The prisoner image recurs in the story just as it did in *The House of Mirth*. Many years earlier, when Ethan realizes he cannot escape his marriage to Zeena, Edith Wharton tells us:

> *The inexorable facts closed in on him like prison-warders handcuffing a convict. There was no way out—none. He was a prisoner for life. . . .*[3]

Indeed, Ethan had always felt trapped in the ramshackle farmhouse where he had grown up. Edith Wharton was a master at setting a scene and giving her readers a distinct sense of place. Her description of the Frome homestead in the dead of a brutal New England winter, which broods over the entire novella, is a memorable example.

> . . . above the fields, huddled against the white immensities of land and sky, [was] one of those lonely New England farmhouses that make the landscape lonelier. . . . The snow had ceased, and a flash of watery sunlight exposed the house on the slope in all its plaintive ugliness. The black wrath of a deciduous creeper flapped from the porch, and the thin wooden walls, under their worn coat of paint, seemed to shiver in the wind that had risen with the ceasing of the snow.[4]

For years, Ethan had longed to leave this life of desolation for something better that he knew lay beyond the horizon. "He had always wanted to be an engineer, and to live in towns, where there were lectures and big libraries and 'fellows doing things.'"[5] In fact Edith portrays Ethan Frome as a man of deep sensitivity, someone in tune with the natural rhythms of the world, interested in looking at the constellations in the night sky. But he is also paralyzed by inaction, much like many of the young men in Edith's own circle and the other male characters in her novels. Indeed, as he passes the headstones that mark generations of Fromes in the family graveyard, they seem to mock him. "We never got away—how should you?"[6]

Only the coming of Zeena's cousin, Mattie Silver, seems to offer Ethan the hope of some relief. But as his love for Mattie grows, Ethan becomes more and more tongue-tied, afraid to express even the smallest hint of his feelings for her. In fact, Ethan is trapped in silence. His father's death had forced him to run the farm alone, with no one to talk to him. Then his mother, who had always been a garrulous woman, fell ill and stopped talking. At first, his cousin, Zeena, had filled the void. But eventually their marriage had become an empty shell, filled with little else but silence.

One day Zeena announces that she is leaving overnight to seek the advice of a new doctor in a nearby town—something she does regularly in search of a magic cure for her imagined illnesses. For the first time, Ethan and Mattie are to be left alone in the house, and his heart suddenly begins to leap in anticipation. The depressing air and winter cold that had hung over the Frome homestead seem to have vanished. Mattie prepares a hearty supper for Ethan and carefully sets the table, even bringing down Zeena's prized pickle dish, which she kept tucked away for special occasions. But as Ethan returns home from his day's work and meets Mattie at the door, he imagines it is Zeena. Although the image immediately disappears, Edith Wharton writes that Ethan is now "suffocated with the sense of well-being."[7] Images of darkness, death, and foreboding abound throughout the entire novel.

While the dinner begins light-heartedly enough for Mattie and Ethan, it is rapidly overtaken by the silence that seems to fill every part of their relationship. "He kept his eyes fixed on her, marveling at the way her face changed with each turn of their talk, like a wheat-field under a summer breeze."[8] But Ethan never expresses his feelings for Mattie, and "when the door of her room had closed on her he remembered that he had not even touched her hand."[9]

The next day Zeena returns and announces to Ethan that the doctor has ordered her to have a complete rest. Consequently, she wants to send Mattie away, because she is a poor housekeeper, and replace her with a hired girl Zeena has already engaged for the job. Suddenly Ethan comes face to face with the utter horror of his predicament and the terrible realization that he is powerless to change it:

> *It was the sense of his helplessness that sharpened his antipathy. There had never been anything in her that one could appeal to, but as long as he could ignore and command he had remained indifferent. Now she had mastered him and he abhorred her. . . . She had taken everything else from him; and now she meant to take the one thing that made up for all the others.*[10]

That night, while Zeena remains in her room, Ethan and Mattie eat dinner together. At this moment of overwhelming sorrow, he finally takes her in his arms and kisses her. But beyond that, what is he to do? The next day Ethan determines to leave Zeena and run off with Mattie to the West. But he soon realizes that he lacks even the money for a train ride. Ethan then decides to call in the payment due to him for a load of lumber he had recently delivered. On the way to collect, he is overcome with guilt at leaving Zeena. Finally, he is forced to confront the fact that he must yield once again to Zeena's wishes and drive Mattie to the train station for her journey away from him.

Mattie conceives a way for them to end their misery, and she convinces Ethan to participate with her in a double suicide. Even at the end, he seems to give up control to someone else. But, of course, the suicide attempt is botched, and the lovers must spend the rest of their lives in abject misery. Edith Wharton thus leaves us with a powerful lesson: Illicit love ends only in disaster.

Ethan Frome first appeared in installments in *Scribner's* magazine, then as a book in 1911. Henry James praised it, and the critics generally agreed. Nevertheless, sales of the book did not match Edith's earlier masterpiece, *The House of Mirth*. Although the sales of *Ethan Frome* may not have been initially impressive, the novella has continued to sell steadily ever since its publication. It is this recognized masterpiece, probably more than any of her other works, that has made Edith Wharton one of the best-known American authors of the twentieth century.

8

ENDINGS AND BEGINNINGS

Soon after publishing *Ethan Frome,* Edith Wharton wrote a short story, *Autres Temps . . .* that describes the plight of Mrs. Lidcote, a society matron who had scandalized old New York when she and her husband divorced. Mrs. Lidcote escaped to Europe and the safety of a small apartment in Florence, only to be summoned home two decades later by a letter from her daughter, Leila, announcing that she, too, had divorced and then remarried. Mrs. Lidcote rushes back to New York, fearing that Leila will suffer the same fate that had befallen her, namely social ostracism. But no sooner does she step foot in America than she learns from Leila's friends that times have changed. As one of them explains: ". . . every woman had a right to happiness and . . . self-expression was the highest duty."[1] For every woman, that is, except Mrs. Lidcote, who learns much to her dismay, that she is still treated as a social outcast. As she so frankly puts it:

> *"Probably no one in the house with me stopped to consider that my case and Leila's were identical. They only remem-*

*bered that I'd done something which, at the time I did it, was
condemned by society. My case had been passed on and classi-
fied: I'm the woman who has been cut for nearly twenty
years. The older people have half-forgotten why, and the
younger ones have never really known: it's simply become a
tradition to cut me. And traditions that have lost their meaning are the hardest of all to destroy."[2]*

For Edith Wharton, the traditions surrounding divorce
were also hard to destroy. She had grown up in an age when
divorce was unacceptable, and although times had surely
changed, she still had mixed feelings about it. Nevertheless, she
was gradually being forced to confront the harsh reality that
she would have to divorce Teddy.

His trip around the world had done nothing to improve
Teddy's state of mind, and as soon as he returned to Paris, all
the old conflicts surfaced again. For years, Teddy's primary
occupation in life had been to manage Edith's money, and he
begged to continue doing it—and preserve his sense of self-
respect—even though he also realized that he was really too
sick to carry on any longer. Edith resisted his pleas, and eventually Teddy left France and sailed for Boston where he
intended to resume the treatments for his mental illness. Once
there, however, he tried to take control of Edith's financial
affairs behind her back, and she felt it necessary to write him
that under no circumstances could he assume his former role.

In July 1911, Edith returned to The Mount. Among her
visitors that summer was her old friend Henry James. Earlier
that year, Edith had fervently hoped the Nobel Prize for literature might be awarded to James. She had even tried to orga-
nize a groundswell of support among her literary friends—
without James's knowledge—to influence the awards
committee. But all to no avail: The prize had gone to some-

one else. Teddy Wharton had been away on a fishing trip during much of James's stay at The Mount, but when he returned, his behavior only increased the discomfort caused by a merciless heat wave enveloping the Berkshires. The arguments between the Whartons again centered around Teddy's desire to manage Edith's estate and her continued resistance to his pleas. She was also planning to sell The Mount, which came as another blow to Teddy, who had been overseeing it for many years while Edith was in Europe.

After investing so much of herself in The Mount, the decision to sell it must have been extremely difficult for Edith. Indeed, she would change her mind more than once before finally giving up a home where she had spent so many wonderful hours and written some of her most important work. But in the end, she recognized the need to make an absolute break with the past, and that included not only leaving The Mount, but also leaving Teddy.

The Whartons' separation did not occur immediately. In the fall, Edith returned alone to Europe and began a whirlwind round of traveling. Accompanied by friend Walter Berry, she motored across northern Italy, visiting some of her favorite cities—Parma, Mantua, Verona, and Florence. In December, Edith was in London, dining with Henry James and visiting old friends. Teddy finally arrived in Paris that winter, but his condition had not improved. During her long ordeal with Teddy Wharton, Edith had the complete support of her friends in Paris—including Morton Fullerton, who had remained a trusted friend long after their love affair had ended. From England, an ailing Henry James also empathized with Edith's predicament.

Eventually, Teddy returned to America, and Edith continued her non-stop schedule of travel and visits with her friends. In the spring, she and Walter Berry returned to Italy. Then it was back to London for the social season, which Edith entered into with her usual intensity. The high point of the season was the Derby for thoroughbred racehorses at Ascot, which over the years had become a fashion show for all the aristocratic women in Britain. There were also lengthy formal dinners, evenings at the opera, and lavish balls that lasted till the wee hours. Then, after the London summer became too hot, the aristocrats left for their country estates where they hosted all their friends at week-long house parties.

One of the most famous country houses in England was Cliveden—the estate of Nancy and Waldorf Astor. Edith traveled there in the summer of 1912 with Henry James dutifully in tow. Unfortunately, Edith's and James's stay at Cliveden that summer ended in misfortune, as James suffered a heart attack that left him terrified and Edith in a frenzy. Even after she left England, Edith's hectic pace continued. She motored to the south of France where she spent a week visiting friends and then continued onto Italy. All this traveling, however, could not prevent Edith from confronting her relationship with Teddy. He had spent the entire year in America, but when Edith suggested she might meet him over there, Teddy warned her not to come. Finally, he sailed for London but seemed no more willing to see Edith there than before. Clearly, he seemed happier apart from her, and Edith brought herself to the painful conclusion that their marriage had reached its end. The divorce decree was finally granted in the spring of 1913. "It's all settled!" she wrote to her friend Gaillard Lapsley, adding, "Now at last [I] know how tired I am!"[3]

9

THE REEF

During the last difficult year of her marriage to Teddy, Edith once again found a release through her writing. In 1912, she published a new novel, *The Reef.* In this novel Edith returned to one of her favorite themes: A woman—Anna Leath—discovers that the man she loves is not everything she thought he was and must decide how to deal with her disappointment. The man in question is a handsome American diplomat, George Darrow. As the story opens, Darrow receives a letter from Anna, whom he hopes to marry, which forces the postponement of their betrothal. With unseemly haste, Darrow seeks consolation in the arms of an attractive young woman Sophy Viner, whom he accidentally meets at a railroad station. Although their relationship lasts only a week, it will have disastrous consequences. As Darrow later admits: "It seemed such a slight thing—all on the surface—and I've gone aground on it because it *was* on the surface."[1] This is the reef from which the novel draws its title.

In *The Reef,* as she had done in *Ethan Frome,* Edith uses flashbacks to tell her story. In one of these flashbacks, Anna recalls her first meeting with George Darrow, which had occurred many years earlier. As Edith wrote: ". . . his passion swept over her like a wind that shakes the roof of the forest without reaching its still glades or rippling its hidden pools."[2] Since Anna does not know how to deal with such strong emotions, Darrow eventually drifts away, and she settles instead for a loveless marriage to Fraser Leath—an American living in France.

Anna is initially won over by Leath's European sophistication, only to realize as his "symmetrical blond mask bent over hers, and his kiss dropped on her like a cold, smooth pebble," that he is totally devoid of any feeling.[3] Instead of love, Anna finds that she has become trapped in her husband's narrow world with its petty prejudices. Even their child, Effie, does not bring Anna and her husband closer together. Anna's only real friend seems to be her stepson, Owen, who shares her sense of imprisonment.

Fraser Leath's unexpected death suddenly releases Anna, and a chance meeting with George Darrow enables her to renew their relationship. Although Anna puts him off at first, Darrow eventually arrives at her chateau where their love affair blossoms. Edith Wharton's description of the chateau on Darrow's first morning there reflects Anna's emotional excitement and is one of the finest passages in the novel:

> It was the day after Darrow's arrival, and he had come down early, drawn by the sweetness of the light on the lawns and gardens below his window. Anna had heard the echo of his step on the stairs, his pause in the stone-flagged hall, his voice as he asked a servant where to find her. She was at the end of the house, in the brown-panelled sitting-room which she frequented at that season because it caught the sunlight first and kept it longest. She stood near the window, in the pale band

of brightness, arranging some salmon-pink geraniums in a
shallow porcelain bowl. Every sensation of touch and sight
was thrice-alive in her. The grey-green fur of the geranium
leaves caressed her fingers and the sunlight wavering across the
irregular surface of the old parquet floor made it seem as bright
and shifting as the brown bed of a stream.[4]

Suddenly Anna experiences an uncomfortable deja vu, as
she recalls how her late husband used to march through the
same rooms. Fortunately for Anna, the ghost of her dead husband quickly evaporates, and she can fully experience her deep
feelings for George Darrow. On his part, Darrow seems to
return Anna's love. His affair with Sophy Viner now long for-
gotten, he seems enraptured at the prospect of spending his life
with Anna.

But as Edith Wharton continually reminds us, the sins of
the past often have an uncomfortable way of jeopardizing the
joys of the present. Darrow's blissful romance with Anna suddenly seems in jeopardy when he comes face to face with her
daughter Effie's beautiful, young governess, who is none other
than Sophy Viner. Because he feels some responsibility to
Sophy, Darrow agrees to keep their affair secret. But he is
clearly appalled that a woman like Sophy should be in charge
of Anna's little girl. He resolves to find her a job somewhere
else. Instead of telling Sophy exactly how he feels about the
situation, Darrow tries to make her think that he wants to help
her. However, Sophy immediately sees through his dishonesty
and recognizes the difficult choice confronting her:

". . . you might naturally feel yourself justified in telling
[Anna] that you don't think I'm the right person for Effie."
He uttered a sound of protest, but she disregarded it. "I don't
say you'd like to do it. You wouldn't: you'd hate it. And the

natural alternative would be to try to persuade me that I'd be better off somewhere else, than here. But supposing that failed, and you saw I was determined to stay? Then you might think it your duty to tell Mrs. Leath."

She laid the case before him with a cold lucidity. "I should, in your place, I believe," she ended with a little laugh.[5]

Darrow's situation becomes even more uncomfortable when he discovers that in addition to caring for Anna's daughter, Sophy is also to marry Anna's stepson, Owen. In a classic case of applying a double standard to men and women, Darrow sees no similarity between Sophy's situation and his own. Although both of them were involved in an affair, only she is to blame, and he redoubles his efforts to remove her from the chateau. Finally, Sophy agrees to call off the marriage without telling Owen the real reason. But he suspects that Darrow is somehow to blame, for he has seen Sophy and Darrow talking to each other on several occasions. When Anna confronts Darrow with this accusation, he sticks to the story that he has told her all along—that Sophy was simply a passing acquaintance from before, and he has been spending time with her at the chateau only to find out if she is suitable to marry Owen. Anna seems to believe him, but she insists that Darrow talk to Sophy once more and prevail upon her to soothe Owen's disappointment. In this tragic confrontation, Darrow learns that an affair that meant so little to him had a quite different meaning to Sophy—she had fallen in love with him, and that is the reason she cannot marry Owen. Sophy's leaving, however, comes too late to preserve Darrow's secret. For Anna at last suspects that there was more between them than simply a casual acquaintance. But even then Darrow doesn't tell Anna the full extent of the relationship. Anna believes that Darrow had only befriended Sophy and helped her financially, and that she had mistaken his intentions and fallen in love with him.

Once Anna learns the true extent of Darrow's relationship with Sophy, she experiences the terrible pain of having been betrayed. Although she still has strong feelings for him, she can't stand to be in his presence. "The Darrow she worshipped was inseparable from the Darrow she abhorred," Edith Wharton wrote, "and the inevitable conclusion was that both must go, and she be left in the desert of a sorrow without memories. . . ."[6] For Anna, life had been simple—a simple love and a simple trust in a man who seemed to embody everything she had wanted. Now she had come face to face with the fundamental complexity of life, but in the painful process, she had also grown psychologically. As Edith Wharton once put it: "I am never interested in the misfortunes of my personages, only in their psychological evolution."[7] And for Anna Leath, this evolution is profound.

Although Anna's thoughts tell her she should reject Darrow, her passions tell her that she cannot live without him, and finally she agrees to become his wife. But their relationship can never be the same again because of Darrow's moral cowardice and duplicity. For as Edith Wharton so succinctly stated, Anna "reflected with a chill of fear that she would never again know if he were speaking the truth or not."[8] This is the realization of a wiser, yet sadder, woman who has resigned herself to a marriage that will be far less than she had hoped it would be.

When *The Reef* was completed, Henry James praised it, and with its tight focus on only four characters, the novel is similar to some of James's best-known works, such as *The Golden Bowl*. But the critics generally agreed that *The Reef* lacked the power of Edith's earlier novels. Sales of the book lagged, and it never measured up to the success of her previous works. Although the novel appears to be semiautobiographical, presenting the conflicting emotions that Edith herself may have experienced in her own relationships, she did not seem very satisfied with the results of her writing.

10

The Custom of the Country

Edith Wharton's disappointment with *The Reef* represents only a brief dip in the road along her long and brilliant literary career. Her next novel, *The Custom of the Country,* received a much warmer reception from the critics and is generally considered one of her greatest works. It was written in fits and starts, beginning in 1908, set aside while Edith finished other novels and short stories, then taken up again, and finally completed. For the then huge sum of $12,500, Charles Scribner bought the serial rights to the novel and ran it in regular installments in *Scribner's* magazine before releasing it in book form during the latter part of 1913.

The novel travels back and forth across the Atlantic between America and France, as it satirizes the customs of the wealthy of both countries. No one understood the social setting of the American and French upper classes better than Edith Wharton. From the vantage point of her apartment in Paris, Edith observed a culture tightly bound by time-honored conventions and prejudices, where a man often felt a far greater loyalty to his mother than he did to his wife, where a

In many of her novels, Edith Wharton describes in detail the interiors of the homes of the well-to-do. This room dates from the 1890s.

married woman was expected to remain subordinate to her husband and choose only those friends who met with his approval, and where even the merest hint of divorce was considered a scandal.

The social customs of aristocratic Paris were not far different from those of old New York where Edith had lived as a child. Indeed, they were still maintained by many of the old Knickerbocker families. With generations of wealth behind them, they considered any discussion of money to be crass, and they even frowned on work. "For four or five generations it had been the rule," as Edith Wharton wrote of one of the families in *The Custom of the Country,* "that a young fellow should go to Columbia or Harvard, read law, and then lapse into more or less cultivated inaction. The only essential was that he should live 'like a gentleman'—that is, with a tranquil disdain for mere money-getting, [and] a passive openness to the finer sensations. . . ."[1]

But by the end of the nineteenth century, these families no longer dominated New York society. The new millionaires— the "invaders," as Edith Wharton called them—with names such as Rockefeller, Havemeyer, Gould, Thaw, and Stevens— had taken over and pushed aside the older aristocracy. For these nouveaux riches, the only thing that seemed important was money and all that it could buy—homes, automobiles, clothes, and, finally, people. The new millionaires wanted to marry into the old aristocracy to gain legitimacy, and the old Knickerbocker families were willing to go along because they wanted money. As Edith Wharton wrote, the daughters of the old New York families "sold themselves to the Invaders; the daughters of the Invaders bought their husbands as they bought an opera box. It ought all to have been transacted on the stock exchange."[2] These American women expected to be indulged, lavished, and if they were not, more and more of them were resorting to the divorce courts so they could look for new husbands with enough money to give them every-thing they wanted.

This is the real focus of *The Custom of the Country*—the conflict of values in turn-of-the-century New York between the old Knickerbocker families and the Invaders, as well as the clash of American and French cultures. At the center of this turmoil, Edith Wharton places one of the most unforgettable heroines in American literature—Undine Spragg. If Lily Bart was the victim of society, then society, in its turn, was victim-ized by Undine Spragg. No more willful, selfish yet endlessly fascinating character has ever been created by an American author. Undine is married four times on two continents, she drives her parents into poverty, shamelessly neglects her only son, and hounds one of her husbands into suicide—all in her unending pursuit of amusement, the admiration of her peers, and a limitless supply of money. But even when she finally achieves them at the novel's conclusion, Undine is still dissatisfied. For there is no substance to her. Happiness must come from inside each person; it cannot be purchased with money, as Edith Wharton well knew. So she condemns Undine to a search that will never end.

Just as she did in *The House of Mirth,* Edith Wharton opens her novel with the central character. Even when Undine Spragg is not directly on stage, her incorrigible behavior drives the story from beginning to end. We are first introduced to the Spraggs after they have made a substantial amount of money and moved East to the pretentious Hotel Stentorian in New York City. With her keen eye for setting and her taste for delicious satire, Edith Wharton wrote:

> *Mrs. Spragg and her visitor were enthroned in two heavy gilt armchairs in one of the private drawing-rooms of the Hotel Stentorian . . . the drawing-room walls, above their wainscoting of highly varnished mahogany, were hung with salmon-pink damask and adorned with oval portraits of Marie Antoinette and Princess de Lamballe. In the center of the florid carpet a gilt table with a top of Mexican onyx sustained a palm in a gilt basket tied with a pink bow. . . . the room showed no traces of human use, and Mrs. Spragg herself wore as complete an air of detachment as if she had been a wax figure in a show-window. Her attire was fashionable enough to justify such a post, and her pale soft-cheeked face, with puffy eyelids and drooping mouth, suggested a partially melted wax figure which had run to double-chin.*[3]

Although the Spraggs had tried to break into New York society, they have so far been unsuccessful—at least until Undine meets Ralph Marvel, the scion of an old Knickerbocker family, who is immediately smitten by her beauty and invites her to one of his parties.

Undine only seems to come to life when she is the center of attention—when she can make a grand entrance to the admiration of those who are in awe of her beauty. But as someone reminds her, to really be accepted by society, "a woman has got to be something more than good-looking . . . she's got to know what's being said about things."[4] Unfortunately, Undine can barely understand the conversations about books and paintings at Ralph's party, and she seems completely out of place among his family and friends. Nevertheless, she has set her sights on marrying someone in high society, and she comes up with a plan to ensure that she is seen by the right people in the right place. The very next morning, Undine asks her father to buy her a box at the opera where all the fashionable New Yorkers will be in attendance. And even when he explains how expensive an opera box is, Undine will not be undone. The combination of her indomitable will and her obvious feminine charms proves more than a match not only for Undine's father but for Ralph Marvel, as well. Ralph is one of Edith Wharton's typical male heroes—weak and ineffectual.

While Ralph is fully aware of Undine's crass tastes, he believes that once they are married he can educate and refine her. But he lacks the strength, and almost from the start he must face the awful realization that he and Undine are totally incompatible. During their honeymoon in Europe, while Ralph is investigating ancient ruins and gazing at the moon, Undine's only interest is in attending balls and concerts and spending huge sums of money. Unfortunately, Ralph's income is too meager to support his wife's lifestyle, and the couple must depend on monthly checks from Undine's father. When this source dries up after Mr. Spragg loses money on Wall Street, Undine lashes out in a childish fit of rage, because her desire to remain in Europe is about to be thwarted.

> *"Your poor father! It's a hard knock for him. I'm sorry,"* [Ralph] *said. . . .*
>
> *For a moment she did not seem to hear; then she said between her teeth: "It's hard for us. I suppose now we'll have to go straight home."*
>
> *". . . I'm so awfully sorry, dearest. It's my fault for persuading you to marry a pauper."*
>
> *"It's father's fault. Why on earth did he go and speculate? There's no use his saying he's sorry now!" She sat brooding for a moment and then suddenly took Ralph's hand. "Couldn't your people do something—help us out just this once, I mean?"*
>
> *He flushed to the forehead: it seemed inconceivable that she should make such a suggestion.*
>
> *"I couldn't ask them—it's not possible. My grandfather does as much as he can for me, and my mother has nothing but what he gives her."*
>
> *Undine seemed unconscious of his embarrassment. "He doesn't give us nearly as much as father does," she said; and, as Ralph remained silent, she went on: "Couldn't you ask your sister, then? I must have some clothes to go home in."*
>
> *His heart contracted as he looked at her. What sinister change came over her when her will was crossed? She seemed to grow inaccessible, implacable—her eyes were like the eyes of an enemy.*[5]

But Ralph gives in and prevails on his sister to send him money. Then after his return to New York, he gives up his position in a law firm and takes a job in real estate to earn a larger income that will satisfy Undine. Totally unsuited to this line of work, Ralph fails at it and becomes even more miserable. Meanwhile, Undine is busy running up larger bills and accepting money to pay for her extravagance from a wealthy admirer—Peter Van Degen—one of the newly rich. In her craving to have all that Van Degen can give her, Undine recognizes how dissatisfied she is with her marriage. She goes to work on a plan to divorce Ralph and marry Van Degen. Although she eventually obtains her divorce, the plan backfires when Van Degen refuses to leave his own wife, and Undine temporarily becomes branded as a social outcast.

A lesser character might have been defeated by these circumstances, but not Undine Spragg. "Her one desire was to get back an equivalent of the precise value she had lost in ceasing to be Ralph Marvel's wife. . . . Her restricted means, her vacant days, all the minor irritations of her life, were nothing compared to this sense of a lost advantage."[6] Edith Wharton describes Undine's situation in business terms, as if she were a financier on Wall Street. And these financial images recur throughout the novel. Edith left no doubt that money had helped destroy Undine's marriage to Ralph and drove her into the arms of Peter Van Degen. When Undine ran short of funds after her divorce she sold an expensive pearl necklace that Van Degen had given her to finance a new life for herself in Paris. And once again, money becomes a key issue, as Undine and Ralph fight over custody of their son, Paul.

Although the court had awarded sole custody of her son to Undine, which was traditional in such cases, she had no interest in Paul, and he remained in New York with Ralph, becoming the center of his father's life. Then Undine decides to remove that center—or at least threaten to remove it—unless Ralph agrees to pay her what she wants. Ralph sets out to raise the necessary money, by borrowing as much as possible from his family, then investing it with Elmer Moffatt, a financier of questionable reputation who promises Ralph a quick return on his investment. When the investment turns sour, Ralph becomes so disconsolate over the prospect of losing his son as well as his family's money that he commits suicide.

Undine, of course, sheds few tears over Ralph's death—she has been far too busy acquiring another husband. Raymond de Chelles is the oldest son of an ancient French aristocratic family with both the name and the inherited wealth to provide Undine with the "two things which she believed should subsist together in any well-ordered life: amusement and respectability."[7] But no sooner does Undine have de Chelles, than she begins to realize that she no longer wants him. While Undine could twist Ralph Marvel around her little finger, Raymond de Chelles is not prepared to give into her whims. In France, women did not have the freedom they were used to enjoying in America, and de Chelles expects Undine to obey his wishes when he tells her which people she can and cannot see. Worst of all, he spends so much money on maintaining his estates to preserve them for the next generation that there is very little left for Undine to spend on herself.

When Undine suggests that her husband sell some of the family heirlooms so she can afford to amuse herself in Paris, he is appalled. De Chelles angrily denounces an entire generation of American women who had come to France seeking husbands without ever bothering to understand the customs of their adopted country:

> "And you're all alike," he exclaimed, "every one of you. You come among us from a country we don't know, and can't imagine, a country you care for so little that before you've been a day in ours you've forgotten the very house you were born in

. . . you come from hotels as big as towns, and from towns as flimsy as paper, where the streets haven't had time to be named, and the buildings are demolished before they're dry, and the people are as proud of changing as we are of holding to what we have—and we're fools to imagine that because you copy our ways and pick up our slang you understand anything about the things that make life decent and honorable for us!" [8]

Not surprisingly, Undine is totally uninterested in trying to improve her understanding of her husband's culture. Instead, she decides to leave him for yet another man who seems far more to her taste—Elmer Moffatt. As it turns out, Moffatt not only becomes Undine's fourth husband, he was also her first— a short-lived affair that was ended by her parents because she was too young and Moffatt had too few prospects of success. But over the years, his dogged persistence and shady manipulations have paid off. Moffatt has accumulated untold millions and spends lavishly on every material possession that Undine could ever hope to own.

It seems like the perfect marriage, but once again Edith Wharton reminds us that the Undine Spraggs of the world are fated never to be satisfied. "Even now, however, she was not always happy. She had everything she wanted, but she still felt, at times, that there were other things she might want if she knew about them. And there had been moments lately when she had had to confess to herself that Moffatt did not fit into the picture." [9]

11

WAR!

In 1913, the same year that *The Custom of the Country* was published, Henry James turned seventy. Edith Wharton placed a very high value on friendship, maintaining close personal relationships with some of the same people for several decades, and none of them was more important to her than Henry James. Edith suspected that Henry had been experiencing financial difficulties, so she wrote a letter to his American friends—including Sara Norton, Egerton Winthrop, and Charles Scribner—asking them to make a contribution to a birthday gift for James, "a sum of money (not less than $5,000) for the purchase of a gift, the choice of which would be left to him."[1] Unfortunately, James got wind of the scheme, and he was so appalled that his friends would think him in need of charity that he immediately put a stop to it.

Although she was quite upset with James's reaction, Edith did not allow it to prevent her from helping him. Instead, she contacted Charles Scribner and prevailed on him to give James an unusually large advance on his next novel. Unknown to Henry James, all the money for the advance had been generously contributed by Edith Wharton.

In December, Edith returned to New York City for the
first time in many years to attend the wedding of her niece,
Beatrix Jones. Beatrix, an internationally renowned landscape
gardener, was the daughter of Edith's older brother Freddy and
his wife, Mary Cadwalader (Minnie) Jones. Although the couple had divorced years earlier, Edith had always maintained
very close relations with Minnie, who was also a close friend
of Henry James. Edith was "petted and feasted" by Minnie.
Nevertheless, she felt extremely uncomfortable in New York,
describing it as "that queer rootless life" where, she said, the
people were lacking in depth, although they still took themselves very seriously.[2] It was the world that Edith had satirized
in *The Custom of the Country*.

After arriving back in Paris, she wasted little time in planning a trip to North Africa. The Wharton party—friends, a
maid for Edith, and her chauffeur—landed in Algiers and traveled south to a village in an oasis. Then it was on to Tunis, a
major port in North Africa.

Eventually, Edith returned to the relative calm and safety of
Paris. But no sooner had she arrived than she was off again. In
July, she and Walter Berry set out on a journey to the south of
France and across the Pyrenees into Spain. After her divorce
from Teddy, some of Edith's friends thought that she and Berry
might marry. But while they had enjoyed a deep and satisfying
relationship for many years, neither seemed seriously interested
in marriage. Berry was a confirmed bachelor with numerous
female friends. As for Edith, after one unhappy marriage she
showed very little inclination to try again.

While Edith and Berry motored through Spain that summer of 1914, terrible events in Europe were about to overtake
them. In June 1914, Archduke Franz Ferdinand, the heir to
the Austro-Hungarian empire, had been assassinated in the

Bosnian city of Sarajevo by a young student sympathetic to Serbian nationalism. This killing began a call-to-arms over the next several weeks that would bring the major European powers to the brink of war. Returning home to Paris after their vacation, Edith and Walter Berry spent the night of July 30 at an inn southwest of Paris. ". . . all night I lay listening to the crowds singing the *Marseillaise* [the French national anthem] in the square in front of the hotel. . . . There were moments when I felt as if I had died, and waked up in an unknown world. And so I had. Two days later war was declared."[3]

Edith Wharton and many of her friends thought the war would be short, with a quick victory by France and its allies, Britain and Russia, over Germany and its allies, Austria-Hungary and the Ottoman Empire. They were, of course, sadly mistaken. Instead the war would drag on for four terrible years.

In August 1914, France drafted hundreds of thousands of men into the armed forces to defend the homeland and defeat the Germans. In Paris, boat traffic on the river Seine slowed down, the bustling streets became quiet, and many small shops, restaurants, and hotels closed as men hurried off to join the army. As business declined throughout Paris and other French cities, many young women, including those who made fashionable clothing, were thrown out of work. The president of one of the branches of the French Red Cross contacted Edith and asked if she might be able to help some of these women by opening a workroom for them. With the loan of an apartment and the help of two young friends, Edith organized a workroom for twenty women, who were paid one franc per day. At first, they made lingerie, filling orders that Edith obtained from her friends in Paris and America. Eventually, they would also make supplies for the hospitals and clothing for the wounded soldiers.

In August, Edith decided to leave Paris briefly for a vacation she had planned in England. While she was across the channel, the German armies rolled toward Paris and were only stopped by determined French resistance at the first battle of the Marne in September. Stranded in England as the battle raged, Edith felt like a deserter. Amid the confusion of war, she finally made her way back to Paris only to discover that the woman she had left in charge of the workroom had fled as the Germans approached the city. The shop Edith had set up was closed and all the women thrown out of work. Edith dutifully gathered the women back together and reopened the shop, expanding its operations as more and more orders poured in.

Edith also expanded her war efforts in other areas. As she wrote to Sara Norton: "The sadness of all things is beyond words, and hard work is the only escape from it."[4] With the same energy that had characterized so much of her life, Edith organized the American Hostels for Refugees to provide homes for families who had been displaced by the war. Refugees were housed at various buildings throughout Paris—some in free furnished rooms, others in apartments where the rents had been reduced to only a nominal charge. In addition, Edith organized a service to provide meals to many refugees, set up a free clinic, and a system for distributing clothes that came in through her contacts in Paris and America. Edith Wharton Committees were established in Philadelphia, in Boston, and in New York City.

In Paris, Edith enlisted the aid of many close friends in the relief work, including the author André Gide, Percy Lubbock, as well as Elisina and Royall Tyler, a couple she had first met in 1912. Elisina was a strikingly beautiful woman, and her husband was an art historian. The Tylers also had a son, William, and although Edith had never been overly fond of small children, William apparently became an exception. In a warm letter written to him on his birthday, Edith regrets that she cannot be there to celebrate with him. "As I cannot come, however, I am sending a little pet to replace me, and as he is very handsome and most beautifully dressed I am almost sure he will remind you of me. As you know, parrots talk, and I have asked this one to give you my love and wish you a great many happy returns of the day."[5]

Elisina Tyler worked tirelessly alongside Edith in establishing the Children of Flanders Rescue Committee. The committee took in refugee children from Belgium, providing them with food, clothing, and shelter. There were classes in French, as well as lace-making for the older girls so they could learn an occupation. Edith even tried to raise enough money so the boys could receive some basic training in industrial arts.

In 1915, Edith began a series of trips to the war zone to deliver hospital supplies and find out firsthand what else the hospitals needed. After the initial battles of the war, the Allies and the Germans had settled down to a grueling ordeal of trench warfare along a front that stretched from the Belgian coast across northern France to Switzerland. It was a stalemate, with one side attacking a position here or storming a fortress there, gaining a few hundred yards of territory, only to lose it again at the cost of hundreds of thousands of casualties. Accompanied by Walter Berry, Edith courageously rode into the thick of the fighting along the Western Front risking her own safety to deliver hospital supplies. In a letter to Henry James, Edith describes one of the battles she witnessed:

> Suddenly we heard the cannon roaring close by, & a woman rushed in to say that we could see the fighting from the back of a house across the street. We tore over, & there, from a garden we looked across the valley to a height about 5 miles

France, 1918. The chaos of war is shown in this photograph of American troops moving to the front. Edith Wharton spent the war years in France providing relief for refugees and others.

away, where white puffs & scarlet flashes kept springing up all over the dark hillside. It was the hill above Vauquois, where there had been desperate fighting for two days. The Germans were firing from the top at the French trenches below (hidden from us by an intervening rise of the ground); & the French were assaulting, & their puffs & flashes were half way up the hill. And so we saw the reason why there are to be so many wounded at Clermont tonight![6]

In another letter to Henry James she described a makeshift hospital:

where beds had been rigged up in two or three little houses, a primitive operating-room installed. Picture this all under a white winter sky, driving great flurries of snow across the mud-&-cinder-coloured landscape. . . . soldiers coming & going, cavalrymen riding up with messages, poor bandaged creatures in rag-bag clothes leaning in doorways, & always, over & above us, the boom, boom, boom of the guns on the grey heights to the east. It was Winter War to the fullest, just in that little insignificant corner of the immense affair![7]

Always the writer, Edith prepared articles on her trips to the front that appeared in *Scribner's* magazine and were later collected in a book, *Fighting France, from Dunkerque to Belfort*, which was published in the fall of 1915. Articles with Edith's byline also appeared in the *New York Times*. Vividly describing her charities in France, they resulted in a large number of donations. In recognition of her outstanding wartime efforts, Edith was made a Chevalier of the Legion of Honor, France's highest award, in 1916. Her compassion and generosity had found an outlet, not in some fashionable drawing room, but amid the horrors of war.

How Edith might have enjoyed a letter from Henry James sending his congratulations. Sadly, none arrived. Henry James had died in February, after suffering a heart attack, followed by a severe stroke. Fortunately, Edith could still gather around her an intimate circle of friends in Paris—Walter Berry, Gaillard Lapsley, Percy Lubbock, Morton Fullerton, Paul and Minnie Bourget, André Gide, and the Tylers. They dined together as often as possible, relying on each other more than ever in a world that was being consumed by the madness of war. Meanwhile, Edith continued her charitable work, lending her support to a program designed to fight tuberculosis, which had broken out among French soldiers fighting in the trenches.

She also opened several convalescent homes for civilians and children who had contracted the disease.

Although the war had reduced the amount of time that Edith could devote to her writing, she did manage to publish a novella in 1917, *Summer.* Considered a companion piece to *Ethan Frome,* the setting for the novella is a New England town during the summer. When a young girl named Charity Royall becomes pregnant by her boyfriend, her elderly guardian agrees to marry her and protect her reputation. While the story describes Charity's loss of independence, the most interesting character is really her guardian—Lawyer Royall, a man of considerable strength as well as human frailties.

The war dragged on into a fourth year. During the winter of 1918, Parisians shivered in their homes as they were forced to endure rationing of electricity and coal. Throughout the city there were serious shortages of milk, eggs, and butter. Theaters were closed four days a week, most of the museums had shut down, and automobile traffic had been almost eliminated to preserve scarce supplies of gasoline for the army. Paris was also being bombarded by the Germans' new large artillery guns, called Big Berthas, as well as extensive air attacks from the large Gotha planes. But the worst was yet to come. The Germans had begun a massive spring offensive aimed at knocking France out of the war.

Fortunately, the Allied position had been strengthened by the arrival of American forces, which began landing in Europe after President Woodrow Wilson brought the United States into the war in 1917. Walter Berry had made a series of fiery speeches in France hoping to persuade America to give up its neutrality and join the Allies even sooner. Both he and Edith were clearly relieved to see their countrymen finally take on the responsibility of waging war against the Germans.

The German offensive fell short, and the Allies began to

push the enemy eastward. By November, with its resources fully exhausted, Germany's leaders at last agreed to an armistice. World War I was over.

For Edith Wharton, the war had been a terrible interlude. With so many soldiers and civilians losing their lives around her, Edith had put her own life temporarily on hold. She then took up charitable work with the same determination and matter-of-factness that she had applied to almost everything else in her life, considering it little more than a job that needed to be done. It was an exhausting endeavor—one that might have overwhelmed other women—but Edith undertook it cheerfully. When the war ended, however, she was clearly relieved to leave this stage of her life behind and return to her first love, writing. "Everything I did during the war in the way of charitable work was forced on me by the necessities of the hour," she explained years later, "but always with the sense that others would have done it far better; and my first respite came when I felt free to return to my own work."[8]

12

THE AGE OF INNOCENCE

ollowing the war, Edith returned to work with a new energy, turning out a steady stream of short fiction, articles, essays and novels. Her most famous book was published at the beginning of the 1920s—an acknowledged masterpiece, called *The Age of Innocence*.

For readers who were trying to forget the horrors of World War I, when an entire generation of young men lost their lives on the battlefields of Europe, *The Age of Innocence* provided a welcome relief. It offered them a nostalgic trip back to a simpler, slower age—the gaslight era of New York in the 1870s. This was the period of Edith's youth, when her parents and others like them ruled Knickerbocker society from their fashionable brownstones around Washington Square—the period before the city was corrupted by the nouveaux riches, who Edith satirized in *The Custom of the Country*.

From the vantage point of the 1920s, with its crass materialism, the traditions and values of the 1870s seemed far more dependable, even though New Yorkers in those days were much narrower in their outlook and more intolerant of anything that seemed the least bit unfamiliar.

In her autobiography, Edith explains that in writing *The Age of Innocence,* "I found a momentary escape in going back to my childish memories of a long-vanished America. . . . I showed it chapter by chapter to Walter Berry; and when he had finished reading it he said: 'Yes; it's good. But of course you and I are the only people who will ever read it. We are the last people left who can remember New York and Newport as they were then, and nobody else will be interested.'"[1] But Berry couldn't have been more wrong. The novel became a huge best-seller and earned Edith a considerable amount in royalties. What's more, it also won her the Pulitzer Prize—she became the first woman writer ever to receive the award.

But the awarding of the prize was marked by controversy. The Pulitzer jury had decided to give it to Sinclair Lewis for his novel *Main Street.* However, they were overruled by Columbia University, which sponsored the award, because they thought the Lewis novel was offensive.

In a warm letter to Sinclair Lewis, Edith admitted: "When I discovered that I was being rewarded by one of our leading universities—for uplifting American morals, I confess I *did* despair. Subsequently, when I found the prize should really have been yours, but was withdrawn because your book (I quote from memory) had 'offended a number of prominent persons in the Middle West,' disgust was added to despair. . . . I wish I could talk to you of all this. Is there no chance of your coming to Paris?"[2] Thus began a friendship between Edith Wharton and Sinclair Lewis that would continue for the rest of her life.

———————————— ❧ ————————————

In *The Age of Innocence*, Edith Wharton returned to one of her most enduring themes: illicit love, this time told through the eyes of a lawyer named Newland Archer. Edith describes

Attending the opera was a favorite pastime of the well-to-do New York families described in The Age of Innocence. *The richest families had boxes where they could meet their friends and be seen by others. Very little attention was paid to the performance or to the music.*

Archer as "a dilettante," and a man shaped by the conventions of the society in which he lives. Archer has become engaged to a young woman from his social set, the beautiful May Welland. May represents his ideal of womanhood—pure, noble, innocent, and someone admired by all his associates, a woman Archer is proud to have on his arm for all the society balls, dinners, and other gala events that he expects to attend. Yet, even as he conforms to conventions, Archer regards himself as superior to them and different from the other men he knows who have not read as much or traveled as widely. He prides himself on having a liberal attitude toward women. As he likes to proclaim to his male friends: "Women ought to be free—as free as we are."[3]

Archer's opinions are put to a severe test with the return to New York of Countess Ellen Olenska, May's cousin. After being mistreated by her Polish husband, Countess Olenska has run away from him with the help of his male secretary. For a woman to engage in this type of behavior seems totally unacceptable to the old Knickerbocker families, and when Ellen is bold enough to appear publicly sitting next to May in a box at the opera, heads are turned all over the theater. But Ellen has her defenders, not the least of whom is her grandmother—the redoubtable Mrs. Manson Mingott, one of the wealthiest and most powerful society matrons in the city. Mrs. Mingott shows a fierce independence and a willingness to defy convention when she welcomes Ellen. Archer admires the old woman's spirit, and since he is engaged to marry May, he finds himself defending her cousin, Ellen, even against the criticism of his own family. While he begins as Ellen Olenska's defender, Archer's interest in her gradually grows into something much stronger and deeper. He finds himself attracted by her unusual beauty and her refreshing candor. In contrast to May, who begins to appear dull and predictable to Archer, Ellen does the unexpected. She seems to have little regard for society's mores.

Ironically, the very thing that attracts Archer is creating a conflict for Ellen. She has returned home to New York to find security, and while asserting her independence, she would also like to conform so society will accept her. "I suppose I've lived too independently," she tells Archer, "at any rate, I want to do what you all do—I want to feel cared for and safe."[4] Ellen naively believes that New Yorkers are simpler, more honest, and more willing to accept her than the people she left behind in Europe, but Archer gently tries to help her see the truth:

"I think I understand how you feel," he said. "Still, your family can advise you; explain differences; show you the way."

She lifted her thin black eyebrows. "Is New York such a labyrinth? I thought it so straight up and down—like Fifth Avenue. And with all the cross streets numbered!" She seemed to guess his faint disapproval of this, and added, with the rare smile that enchanted her whole face, "If you knew how I like it for just that—*the straight-up-and-downness, and the big honest labels on everything!"*

He saw his chance. "Everything may be labelled—but everybody is not."

"Perhaps. I may simplify too much—but you'll warn me if I do."[5]

As Archer tries to guide Ellen around the pitfalls of New York society, she unknowingly forces him to see it more critically. When Ellen wants to sue her husband for divorce, the Mingotts ask Archer to dissuade her and thus avoid the scandal it might cause them. But even as he attempts to serve the Mingott interests, Archer's passion and concern for Ellen (and his conflict with the Mingotts) grows stronger.

Unable to deal with this problem, Archer decides to run away to Florida where May is vacationing with her family. At first he is able to delude himself into believing that May is all that he wants and implores her to move up the date of their wedding. But she suspects that his eagerness may be caused by a fear that if he waits too long he will succumb to his feelings for someone else. Indeed, May is far more perceptive than Archer realizes, and in her own way, she proves to be as strong and determined as Ellen Olenska.

After May initially refuses to change the wedding day, Archer finally admits to himself that it is really Ellen he loves and tries to persuade her to obtain a divorce so they can be together. For a moment he holds her in his arms and they kiss. But Ellen has been won over by Archer's previous arguments, and she is far too concerned about hurting May and the rest of her family to give in to him.

Edith Wharton divides *The Age of Innocence* into two sections. Book I ends as Ellen turns down Archer's request and at almost the same moment he receives a telegram from May saying that she has agreed to an earlier date for their marriage. Book II begins with their wedding ceremony and then follows the couple on their honeymoon to Europe. Once outside New York, Archer hopes that he might enlarge May's horizons and introduce her to new ideas. But he soon concludes that this is impossible:

> *In London, nothing interested her but the theatres and the shops. . . . Archer had reverted to all his old inherited ideas about marriage. It was less trouble to conform with the tradition and treat May exactly as all his friends treated their wives than to try to put into practice the theories with which his untrammelled bachelorhood had dallied. There was no use in trying to emancipate a wife who had not the dimmest notion that she was not free. . . .*[6]

Upon their return home, the Archers' lives move predictably between New York City and Newport. In time, Archer wearies of Newport, much as Edith did later in life. He is also feeling trapped by his conventional lifestyle (as in her other novels, images of entrapment appear here). Once more, Ellen seems to offer him his only chance of escape, and he journeys to Boston to find her. Edith Wharton possessed an unusual sensitivity to her surroundings and how they could reflect human emotions, a talent she used time and again in her fiction. When Archer catches up with Ellen, for example, she is sitting on a bench in Boston Common. It is a sweltering day, the perfect setting for the awkward discussion that follows. Ellen tells Archer that her husband has asked her to come home in return for a large sum of money, which she has refused. The couple then try to express their feelings for each other, but without much success, and Archer suggests that they escape the heat for a boat ride in the bay. Here the more pleasant surroundings provide a perfect backdrop to his emotions:

> *As the paddle-wheels began to turn and the wharves and shipping to recede through the veil of heat, it seemed to Archer that everything in the old familiar world of habit was receding also. He longed to ask Madame Olenska if she did not have the same feeling: the feeling that they were starting on some long voyage from which they might never return. But he was afraid to say it, or anything else that might disturb the delicate balance of her trust in him.*[7]

Eventually Edith Wharton brings her characters back to reality. Ellen tells Archer, amidst her sadness and longing for him, that their relationship can be no more than it presently is. While Ellen has tried to find a perfect balance between her feelings for Archer and her responsibilities to May, Edith Wharton reminds us that such an equilibrium is not possible in the real world. May's family has become convinced that Ellen and Archer are having an affair, and are determined to put an end to it. At first, they try to force Ellen to return to Europe and her husband, but when Archer learns of it he suggests, instead, that they should run away together. However, Ellen understands much better than he does what would await them:

> *"I want—I want somehow to get away with you into a world where . . . we shall be simply two human beings who love*

each other, who are the whole of life to each other; and nothing else on earth will matter."

She drew a deep sigh that ended in another laugh. "Oh, my dear—where is that country? Have you ever been there?"

". . . Then what, exactly, is your plan for us?" he asked.

"For us? But there's no us in that sense! We're near each other only if we stay far from each other. Then we can be ourselves. Otherwise we're only Newland Archer, the husband of Ellen Olenska's cousin, and Ellen Olenska, the cousin of Newland Archer's wife, trying to be happy behind the backs of the people who trust them."

"Ah, I'm beyond that," he groaned.

"No, you're not! You've never been beyond. And I have," she said in a strange voice, *"and I know what it looks like there."*[8]

Eventually, Mrs. Manson Mingott rescues her granddaughter, at least temporarily, by inviting Ellen to live under her protection in the Mingott mansion. Then, unknown to Archer, May becomes pregnant with their first child. When she purposely tells Ellen, this is enough to persuade her to leave New York for good.

In a final ceremony to mark Ellen's departure, May holds a farewell party for her with all the members of their social set in attendance. It is a gala event, but one filled with hypocrisy. While each person outwardly smiles at Ellen, inwardly each is delighted to see her go. "There were certain things that had to be done, and if done at all, done handsomely and thoroughly," Edith Wharton tells us, "and one of these, in the old New York code, was the tribal rally around a kinswoman about to be eliminated from the tribe."[9] An individual is sacrificed cruelly and unjustly, Edith Wharton tells us. But the traditional values of marriage and the family are preserved. And these, Edith firmly believed, were the foundation of a stable society.

In its final chapter, *The Age of Innocence* moves ahead in time almost twenty-six years. May has died, and Archer is traveling to Paris with his grown son, Dallas. On her deathbed, May had revealed to Dallas the relationship between his father and Ellen Olenska. In the meantime, Ellen has done a favor for Dallas's fiancée, and the young man decides that he and his father should stop and visit her. Archer reluctantly agrees, although he had not seen Ellen since the night of the party so long ago. But when father and son finally reach her apartment, Archer cannot bring himself to go in. He prefers instead to sit outside and gaze up at her balcony, imagining the woman who would be sitting inside.

13

TRANSITIONS AND THE WRITER'S ART

Although Edith Wharton chose to set the final chapter of *The Age of Innocence* in her beloved Paris, it was a city she had already left behind when the novel was published in 1920. Edith had apparently wearied of the bustle and congestion of urban life and wished to move to the quieter countryside where she could recreate the lifestyle she had enjoyed at The Mount. A short distance north of Paris, she purchased a home—Pavillon Colombe—that had been abandoned during the war and now needed major work done to restore it. At the same time, she was also exploring one of her favorite haunts, Hyères on the French Riviera, with her close friend Robert Norton, a British watercolor painter. Here Edith chanced on a run-down former convent called Ste. Claire, with a fine view overlooking the town. She decided to lease this property for the winters. "I am thrilled to the spine," she wrote Royall Tyler, "and I feel as if I were going to get married—to the right man at last!"[1] Both of these homes required Edith's practiced eye as a designer and landscape gardener, and she energetically set about supervising all the necessary improvements that would make them suitable for her needs.

Pavillon Colombe was one of the French country houses where Edith Wharton spent the last days of her life.

Edith's lifelong love affair with landscape gardening was clearly displayed at Pavillon Colombe, with its quiet goldfish pool and its displays of lush flowers. She had also created beautiful gardens at Ste. Claire. So important were these gardens to her, that Edith spent the $1,000 she received for winning the Pulitzer Prize to refurbish them after a deadly frost.

For the remainder of her life, Edith Wharton would live at Pavillon Colombe during the summer and fall months and at Ste. Claire in the winters. Here she graciously welcomed old friends such as Paul and Minnie Bourget, Rosa de Fitz-James, the art historian Bernard Berenson, André Gide, Walter Berry, and John Hugh Smith, as well as some new, younger people. One day the young American writer, F. Scott Fitzgerald journeyed out to visit Edith at Pavillon Colombe. Edith had written him that she admired his novel *The Great Gatsby*. But Fitzgerald may still have felt anxious about meeting so famous an author, for he had been drinking rather heavily before his arrival. Edith was not happy with the visit of her inebriated guest.

Daily life for Edith often followed a fairly regular routine: work in the morning, lunch, followed by long walks until late afternoon. During the early 1920s, Edith completed several novels, including *The Glimpses of the Moon*, published by Appleton in 1922, and *A Son at the Front*, published the following year by Scribner's. The first novel describes the seemingly aimless lifestyle of a young married couple who live off their friends, while the latter is based directly on Edith's own experiences during World War I. It deals with a soldier who dies on the battlefield, as well as the experiences of his relatives and friends on the homefront in Paris. These and other writings earned Edith an estimated $250,000 between 1920 and 1924. Although it was a large sum, she needed a great deal of money to run two estates with their full staffs of servants, in addition to the cost of entertaining her friends regularly and of her assorted charities.

In 1923, Edith made her first trip to America in ten years. She had been summoned to receive an honorary Doctor of Letters from Yale University. At first she had been hesitant about making the trip but decided it would be ungracious to refuse. In New York, Edith was greeted by family members; then, after visiting with friends, she traveled to New Haven, Connecticut, to receive her honorary degree. A few days later, she was back on the boat, sailing home to Europe.

Traveling continued unabated. In the spring of 1926, Edith

chartered a yacht, and in the company of Robert Norton and several other friends set out on a ten-week cruise that took them across the Ionian Sea, to the Gulf of Corinth, Delphi, and the Aegean. She had taken a similar trip many years earlier with Teddy shortly after they were married. Later that year, Edith was off again—this time with Walter Berry on a journey that took them to northern Italy. The pair visited the walled city of Bergamo perched high atop a hill, whose weathered stone buildings, narrow streets, and cobbled piazzas made visitors feel as if they had been carried back in time to the Middle Ages. Then they traveled southeast to Venice, enjoying a sail along the Grand Canal, with its slumbering villas, before heading out to the long stretch of beach known as the Lido. Unknown to either Edith Wharton or Walter Berry, this would be the last time they would share the splendors of this magical city together.

Upon his return home, Berry suffered a slight stroke. He seemed to improve, however, and eventually came to Ste. Claire to continue his recovery. Then he left for Switzerland to undergo further medical treatment. But in the fall of 1927, Berry was stricken again, this time with a major stroke, at his home in Paris. Edith rushed to his bedside and was with him almost to the end. "Walter died this morning," she wrote a friend. "Yesterday afternoon I held him in my arms, & talked to him of old times, & he pressed my hand and remembered."[2]

For Edith, the loss was irreparable. No one probably knew her better than Walter Berry, no one had meant more to her, no one had probably done as much for her personally and professionally over so many years. In a brief note to friend Gaillard Lapsley, Edith expressed her profound sorrow by stating simply: "All my life goes with him."[3]

In 1927, Edith Wharton was sixty-five, but her advancing age in no way reduced the size of her literary output. That year, for example, she published *Twilight Sleep*—a novel about the aimless lives of a group of wealthy Americans during the 1920s. It immediately became a national best-seller. The book takes its title from the effort to make childbirth painless by giving women anesthesia during delivery. But it was also Edith's way of referring to the way people seemed to go through life in the Twenties—anesthetized to its harsh realities.

A delicious piece of satire, *Twilight Sleep* opens with a humorous characterization of Mrs. Pauline Manford—a woman who tries to fill every waking moment with activity so she will never have to confront the emptiness of her own existence. Pauline is so busy that her own children must make an appointment with her secretary just to see her. "'But look at her list—just for this morning!' the secretary continued, handing over a tall morocco-framed tablet, on which was inscribed in the colorless secretarial hand: '7:00 Mental uplift. 7:54 Breakfast. 8:00 Psychoanalysis. 8:15 Facial massage. 9:00 Man with Persian miniatures. 9:15 Correspondence. 9:30 Manicure. 9:45 Eurythmic exercises.'"[4] The rest of Mrs. Manford's day is filled with her work for an assortment of altruistic causes—the Mother's Day Association, the Birth Control Movement, the Militant Pacifists' League—and her unending search to find happiness through a succession of spiritual healers that include a false Mahatma, a frustration therapist, and a Scientific Initiate who promises to help Pauline smile her problems away.

One of Pauline's major problems is the relationship—or lack of it—with her husband, Dexter Manford, a successful lawyer who has become bored with his daily routine.

The New York routine had closed in on him, and he sometimes felt that, for intrinsic interest, there was little to choose between Pauline's hurry and his own. They seemed, all of them—lawyers, bankers, brokers, railway-directors, and the

rest—to be cheating their inner emptiness with activities as
futile as those of the women they went home to.

It was all wrong—something about it was fundamentally
wrong. They all had colossal plans for acquiring power, and
then, when it was acquired, what came of it but bigger houses,
more food, more motors, more pearls, and more self-righteous
philanthropy?[5]

Dexter tries to escape his boredom in a brief affair with his
beautiful but vapid daughter-in-law, Lita. While her husband is
working endlessly to satisfy her every desire, Lita fills her days
spending his money and complaining that there is never
enough of it. Surveying her magnificent home, Lita moans to
her sister-in-law Nona:

"This room is awful, *isn't it? Now acknowledge that it is!*
And Jim won't give me the money to do it over."

"Do it over? But, Lita, you did it exactly as you pleased
two years ago!"

"Two years ago? Do you mean to say you like anything
that you liked two years ago?"[6]

Lita has already stopped "liking" her husband and wants to
divorce him so she can leave for Hollywood and a career in the
movies.

Nona, Dexter and Pauline's daughter, is the only character
in the novel capable of seeing through the facade of her family's lifestyle. While admiring her mother's energy, Nona also
recognizes that Pauline is a shallow person who is content to
only scratch the surface of life and avoid its unpleasant side.
Nona clearly feels more deeply than the rest of her family. It is
Nona who assumes the responsibility of helping each of them
with their problems. She realizes that their attempts to escape

reality by uninterrupted busyness, incessant traveling, or extra-marital affairs will not make them any happier. While she is looking after everyone else, however, Nona seems unable to find any lasting purpose in her own life. Indeed, *Twilight Sleep* seems to be lacking a clearly defined purpose except to portray the malaise of the 1920s. Although the novel was extremely popular among readers of the period, it does not contain the powerful characterizations or tightly structured plot of Edith Wharton's most successful works.

During the 1920s, Edith Wharton demonstrated her wide range as a writer of novels as diverse as *Twilight Sleep*, *A Son at the Front*, and *The Age of Innocence*. In between, Appleton also published a set of four of Edith's novellas, collectively titled *Old New York*. With each one set in a different era, from the 1840s through the 1870s, they demonstrated once again her enormous talents as storyteller.

The most powerful story in this quartet is *The Old Maid*. When this tale was offered for serialization before being published as a novella, no magazine at first wanted to handle it; the subject of illegitimacy seemed too controversial. Eventually, *The Old Maid* appeared in *Redbook*.

The old maid in the story is Charlotte Lovell, who as a young woman, gave birth to an illegitimate daughter, Tina. When Charlotte reveals this secret to her cousin, Delia Ralston, who is married to one of *the* Ralstons, Delia's secure, uppercrust world suddenly seems on shaky ground. But Delia rises above the conventions of Knickerbocker society and agrees to support Charlotte and her daughter, if they agree to live away from the city. After Delia's husband dies unexpectedly, she invites Charlotte and Tina to live with her. The little girl is raised with Delia's other children and, in fact, calls her "mother," believing that Charlotte is her maiden aunt. Although Charlotte doesn't want Tina to learn about the cir-

cumstances of her birth, she longs to be a mother to her and
resents that Delia plays this role. Many years later, on the night
before Tina's marriage, Charlotte can contain herself no
longer. In a harsh, angry confrontation with Delia, she threat-
ens to tell Tina everything.

> "Do you suppose it's been easy, all these years, to hear her
> call you 'mother'? Oh, I know, I know—it was agreed that
> she must never guess . . . but if you hadn't perpetually come
> between us she'd have had no one but me, she'd have felt
> about me as a child feels about its mother, she'd have had to
> love me better than any one else. With all your forbearances
> and your generosities you've ended by robbing me of my child.
> And I've put up with it all for her sake—because I knew I
> had to. But tonight—tonight she belongs to me. Tonight I
> can't bear that she should call you 'mother'."[7]

In the end, Charlotte Lovell remains silent, knowing that
the truth would destroy her daughter's future. In Tina's mind
she will remain forever *The Old Maid*.

In addition to her novellas, novels, and essays, Edith Wharton wrote more than eighty short stories. She is still considered
one of the finest writers of this genre. In her book, *The Writing
of Fiction*, published in 1925, she explains that a good short
story should be "a shaft driven straight into the heart of experience." As the critic Margaret McDowell adds, Edith believed
that "the author must introduce no irrelevant detail to distract
the reader's attention for a moment. The effect of compactness
and instantaneousness, she thought, would result from the strict
observation of the unity of time and from the use of a single
pair of eyes to focus upon the rapidly enacted episodes."[8]

In *The Temperate Zone*, published in 1924, the story is seen through the eyes of Willis French, a young author doing research on an artist whose works have only become highly prized after his death. In pursuit of more information, French finally secures an interview with the artist's widow, the subject of one of his most admired paintings. Their conversation, however, reveals her to be a frivolous woman who only seems interested in clothes, jewels, and reaping as much money as possible from her husband's works. By chance, French uncovers one of the artist's sketches, while exploring one day in his workshop. His widow, who recognizes the value of any piece of art that was created by her late husband, generously allows French to keep it but in return she asks a favor of him: Would he arrange to have her portrait painted by one of his acquaintances, a well-known painter who is nowhere near as talented as her husband, but whose work is extremely successful because he is patronized by all of society's elite. It is a telling moment, "a shaft driven into the heart of experience," which brilliantly reveals the woman's shallow character.

Some years later, Edith published one of her most powerful short stories, *Roman Fever*. The story describes two middle-aged friends, Grace Ansley and Alida Slade, sitting in a restaurant overlooking the Roman Forum. Their husbands having both died, the two women have come to Rome to accompany their grown daughters who wandered off earlier in the day with some young Italian aviators. Mrs. Ansley and Mrs. Slade then begin to reminisce about their own experiences in Rome when they were the same age. But in the course of this seemingly pleasant conversation, each of them reveals a terrible secret. It appears that Grace Ansley had been in love with Delphin Slade, Alida's husband, during his engagement to her. When Alida discovered their relationship, she forged a letter from Delphin to Grace asking her to meet him near some

ruins just after dark. Since Grace's health was delicate, Alida
hoped that Grace might catch a bad chill if she went out at
night expecting to meet Delphin. "I'd found out," Alida tells
her, "and I hated you, hated you. I knew you were in love
with Delphin—and I was afraid; afraid of you, of your quiet
ways, your sweetness . . . your . . . well, I wanted you out of
the way, that's all. Just for a few weeks; just till I was sure of
him."[9] Since Alida and Delphin were eventually married, she
felt quite smug at being able to outsmart Grace and even more
self-satisfied at finally revealing it to her. But Alida has very
little time to savor her moment of triumph. Although she
assumed all along that Delphin had never shown up to meet
Grace, apparently she had been mistaken.

> Mrs. Ansley's voice grew clearer, and full of surprise. "But of
> course he was there. Naturally he came—"
>
> "Came? How did he know he'd find you there? You must
> be raving!"
>
> Mrs. Ansley hesitated, as though reflecting. "But I
> answered the letter. I told him I'd be there. So he came."
>
> Mrs. Slade flung her hands up to her face. "Oh, God—
> you answered! I never thought of you answering. . . ."
>
> . . . Mrs. Slade gave an unquiet laugh. "Yes; I was beaten
> there. But I oughtn't to begrudge it to you, I suppose. At the
> end of all these years. After all, I had everything; I had him
> for twenty-five years. And you had nothing but that one letter
> that he didn't write."[10]

But Grace Ansley has not yet revealed the final part of her
secret, which only appears in the very last line of the story.
Telling that secret here, however, would only spoil the impact
of *Roman Fever*, which must be completely read to be fully
appreciated.

14

HUDSON RIVER
BRACKETED

66I am overwhelmed by what you say of 'Hudson Riv,'"
Edith wrote her friend Elisina Tyler. "After allowing for
all the indulgence of affection, there seems so much
more praise than the book deserves—yet I wd rather hear it of
this than of any other I have written. It is a theme that I have
carried in my mind for years, & that Walter was always urging
me to use. . . ."[1]

In 1929, Edith Wharton published *Hudson River Bracketed*
and introduced one of her most enduring male characters—
Vance Weston. Vance is an aspiring young writer—much as
Edith had been many years earlier. His struggle to become a
successful novelist, while at the same time trying to deal with
the turmoil of his personal life, form the core of the novel.

The story opens in the Middle West, a favorite target of
Edith Wharton's satire. She pokes fun at its towns, giving them
names like Hallelujah, Advance, and Euphoria; ridicules its
preachers who tout their religion as "the greatest shortcut to
success"; and satirizes the Midwestern value system, with its
emphasis on constantly moving onward and upward. Vance

Weston's father, a real estate speculator, drags his family from one dusty community to another in his continuing search for greater and greater financial rewards. At nineteen, Vance seems to have inherited his father's unsettled outlook. "Vance Weston, in truth, could not dissociate stability from stagnation anymore in religion than in business. All the people he had heard of who hadn't got a move on at the right moment, in whatever direction, were down and out."[2]

Down and out is the perfect way to describe Vance's impoverished cousins, the Tracys. After poor health forces on him a change of climate, Vance travels to their ramshackle home in upper New York State where he must learn to make do with no hot water, no electric lights, and without even that most fundamental of modern conveniences, a telephone. But if the Tracys represent an "absence of initiative which no Euphorian could understand," it soon becomes clear that they also symbolize something else: a firm connection to the past.[3] And Vance needs to make this connection, Edith Wharton tells us, to become a successful writer.

When he first arrives at the Tracys, Vance is experiencing the natural frustrations of a young poet struggling to get something on paper. It is only after he visits the Willows, an old homestead where the Tracys work as caretakers, that Vance begins to find his voice as a writer. Here he discovers the past. Edith Wharton creates the perfect setting for it—the Willows, a grand relic of a once popular style of architecture known as Hudson River Bracketed:

> *When the front of the house was before them, disengaged from the fluctuating veil of willows, Vance saw that it was smaller than he had expected, but the air of fantasy and mystery remained. . . . The shuttered windows were very tall and narrow, and narrow too the balconies, which projected at odd*

angles, supported by ornate wooden brackets. One corner of the house rose into a tower with a high shingled roof, and arched windows which seemed to simulate the openings in a belfry. . . . Vance wandered around to the other side of the building. Here a still stranger spectacle awaited him. An arcaded verandah ran across this front, and all about it, and reaching above it from bracket to bracket, from balcony to balcony, a wisteria with huge distorted branches like rheumatic arms lifted itself to the eaves, festooning, as it mounted, every projecting point with long lilac fringes—as if, Vance thought, a flock of very old monkeys had been ordered to climb up and decorate the house front in celebration of some august arrival.[4]

Once inside the Willows, Vance ultimately settles himself in the library. Here he is introduced to the great literary works of the past, which help him find his own voice as a writer. Here too he meets Heloise (Halo) Spear who will become his muse. The remainder of the novel is told alternately from the viewpoint of Vance and Halo as their lives intertwine, then separate, and finally come back together again.

Halo Spear is one of the most engaging female characters ever created by Edith Wharton. A clear-eyed realist, Halo accepts that she may not have what it takes to be a great artist or writer, but she can recognize and encourage these talents in others. Halo is also very practical, especially when it comes to money, realizing that she can't really be happy without it. Yet, she is no Undine Spragg. Halo hopes to marry for love as well as money. But readers of Edith Wharton's fiction realize by now that a price must be paid for everything. Eventually Halo settles for a loveless marriage to wealthy Lewis Tarrant.

Meanwhile, Vance has gone to New York City where he looks for a job on a newspaper. He soon realizes that only when he writes in his own style (instead of trying to mimic the style of others) and from his own experience does he really have anything worthwhile to say. No one knew this better than Edith Wharton. When Vance submits a short story to *The Hour* magazine based on an incident from his life back home in Euphoria, it is accepted.

The demand for Vance's work increases when, quite by chance, Lewis Tarrant decides to buy *The Hour* and revitalize it. The magazine even submits one of Vance's stories for a Pulsifer Prize, awarded to the year's best short story. With biting satire, Edith Wharton then describes the maneuverings that go on behind the scenes to influence the awarding of the prize. The awards committee, it seems, does not make its decision based strictly on merit, but on the whims of silly, middle-aged Mrs. Pulsifer who sees to it that the prize goes only to the writer who appeals to her roving eye. Unfortunately, Vance is too unsophisticated to handle Mrs. Pulsifer's romantic interest in him and fails to win the award.

Nevertheless, he does succeed in signing a literary contract for his novels and short stories. Edith Wharton gives us a brilliant satire of these contract negotiations. Indeed, *Hudson River Bracketed* is filled with Edith's barbed comments about the entire American literary scene. She ridicules the emptiness of modern best-sellers, pulp fiction writers, and boring literary parties where Vance sadly discovers "everybody talked and nobody listened. . . ."[5]

While Vance is struggling to make a career for himself, he is also suffering through an unhappy marriage to his cousin, Laura Lou Tracy. Like Newland Archer in *The Age of Innocence*, Vance finds himself married to a woman who really doesn't understand what motivates him. In addition, her frail health and repeated illnesses create a burden for Vance, which he finds difficult to bear. Looking at Laura Lou as she lies in bed delirious with fever, he is struck by a startling realization:

At one moment her eyes, which had clung to his so anxiously, always asking for something he could not guess, suddenly became the eyes of a stranger. . . . Was this why we were all so fundamentally alone? Because, as each might blend with another in blissful fusion, so, at any moment, the empty eyes of a stranger might meet us under familiar brows?[6]

Although Vance feels estranged from his wife, he also suffers from a sense of guilt because he cannot afford proper medical care for her, adequate food, or even enough heat for their miserable apartment. But he still refuses to give up his dream of becoming a successful writer. Eventually Vance decides to move Laura Lou back to the security of her family, and he returns to the Willows where he begins to create his most brilliant work of fiction. One day while he is absorbed in his writing, Vance is interrupted by Halo. He begins to read from the pages of his novel:

. . . and after the first paragraph he was swept on by the new emotion of watching his vision take shape in another mind. Such a thing had never happened to him, and before he had read a page he was vibrating with the sense of her exquisite participation. What his imagination had engendered was unfolding and ripening in hers; whatever her final judgment was, it would be as if his own mind had judged him.[7]

Halo returns again and again, inspiring Vance to complete his novel. Although it is hailed as a great success, even this cannot make up for the emptiness of his marriage. Throughout her career, Edith Wharton explored the tragic breakdown in communications between husbands and wives. As she points out in *Hudson River Bracketed*, Vance's feelings of isolation arise not only because Laura Lou doesn't understand him, but, as he admits, "he really knew next to nothing of the secret springs of her thoughts and emotions."[8] Meanwhile Halo has also become disillusioned by her relationship with Tarrant, which she recognizes as nothing more than a marriage of convenience. However, when Vance tells Halo that he has fallen in love with her, she says that they must be content with friendship and nothing more because she does not believe in being unfaithful to her husband.

Vance struggles on alone—overcoming the failure of his next novel and finally beginning a new one. While Vance becomes absorbed in his novel, Laura Lou tries to hide the fact that her health is growing progressively worse. She is in the final stages of tuberculosis, which will ultimately claim her life. As the novel closes, Vance explores his feelings about the two women who have formed so central a part of his life—Laura Lou and Halo Tarrant. Standing outside his miserable bungalow, he talks to Halo about the future. Although he still wants to develop a closer relationship with her, Vance is brought up short by the sudden realization that this may be impossible for the very same reason that his marriage to Laura Lou had failed. With these haunting lines, which perhaps described her own life, Edith Wharton concludes: "And when at last he drew her arm through his and walked beside her in the darkness to the corner where she had left her motor, he wondered if at crucial moments the same veil of unreality would always fall between himself and the soul nearest him, if the creator of imaginary beings must always feel alone among the real ones."[9]

15

THE FINAL YEARS

During the last decade of her life, Edith Wharton filled her days with old friends and new acquaintances, a regular outpouring of literary work, which would have been remarkable for someone half her age, and the usual busy travel schedule that took her to many of the countries of Europe. In the summer of 1929, for example, during her regular visit to England, Edith made a nostalgic return trip to Bodiam Castle south of London. What must have raced through her mind as she stood with Robert Norton, looking across the circular moat and up at the huge stone battlements "wh. Henry first showed me 20 years ago."[1]

During the early 1930s she began writing her autobiography, *A Backward Glance*. Edith busied herself gathering information on the early history of her family and writing to close friends for their recollections of Henry James. She also completed a sequel to *Hudson River Bracketed*, called *The Gods Arrive*. However, reviews of the novel were not encouraging, nor did it ever become a best-seller. Apparently, the American public did not find her newest book quite as appealing as some of her earlier works.

By now, America was in the midst of the Great Depression. Like many other writers, Edith's income was seriously affected. Sales of her previous novels were low. In addition, the popular magazines, which in the past had offered large sums to serialize Edith's stories, were now offering a lot less because their advertising sales were down—another result of the Depression. In a letter to her editor at Appleton, Rutger Jewett, who usually negotiated the serial rights for her books, Edith complained that the *Ladies Home Journal* was trying to go back on a deal they had made for her autobiography:

> . . . it was about three years ago that the L.H.J. offered me $25,000 for my Reminiscences. I accepted on condition that no date was fixed for the delivery of the manuscript, and since then they have been receiving the manuscript from you as it was written, and no comment has been offered on it and no conditions fixed as to its length. I have been working very hard over this book, and cannot consent to have one-fifth of the price offered suddenly cut off. No doubt L.H.J. is hard up, but so am I, and I imagine that they have larger funds to draw upon than I have.[2]

Edith needed money not only to pay the huge costs of running her estates, but also to support her various charities. These included a few close friends who required her help, as well as her sister-in-law, Minnie Jones, who had long depended on Edith's generosity. During this period, Edith helped pay her expenses by publishing several collections of short stories. Perhaps, not surprisingly, some of the most powerful among them dealt with the themes of old age and death.

Edith Wharton at her writing desk.

Explaining the title of one of her most haunting tales, *Pomegranate Seed*, she told Jewett: "When Persephone left the under-world to re-visit her mother, Demeter, her husband, Hades, lord of the infernal regions, gave her a pomegranate seed to eat, because he knew that if he did so she would never be able to remain among the living, but would be drawn back to the company of the dead."[3] In *Pomegranate Seed*, Edith tells the story of Kenneth Ashby, a widower who seems happily settled with his new wife, Charlotte. Only one thing seems to disrupt the couple's marital bliss: After they return from their honeymoon, Ashby begins to receive mysterious letters from Elsie, his deceased first wife. The letters act like a strange magnet, inexorably drawing him to her. One day Ashby disappears never to return.

An exclusive hotel in the Alps is the setting for *Confession*, another of Edith's stories. Here a love affair begins between Severance, who is the narrator of this story, and the fashionable Kate Ingram. Mrs. Ingram, whose real name is Kate Spain, is gradually unmasked as a woman with a checkered past. Accused of murdering her tyrannical father, she was tried and acquitted. But ever since, she has been trying to escape the notoriety caused by the trial. After learning of her true identity, Severance continues to pursue Kate and wants her to become his wife. But her companion, Cassie, stands in the way. Eventually, she is killed by a sudden stroke, just as she is about to make a terrible confession about her mistress. Although Severance finally marries Kate, their life together is short-lived, for she dies five years later.

Other notable stories published during the 1930s include, *After Holbein*, in which Edith presents a senile grand dame who persists in giving elaborate dinner parties although no one ever attends them. Finally, in *Duration*, Edith wittily describes two cousins who have endured for a century and are preparing to mark the occasion at a gala one-hundredth birthday celebration.

Like the characters in her stories, old age was catching up not only with Edith but also with many of her friends and relatives. In 1933, Minnie Jones was already in her eighties. That same year, two of Edith's elderly household staff were stricken and eventually died. One of them—her housekeeper, the ancient and devoted Catherine Gross—had been with Edith since 1884.

Nevertheless, Edith did not allow the feelings of loneliness caused by these deaths to keep her downhearted for long. That summer she motored to Wales with close friend Gaillard Lapsley, himself over sixty. Then she was on to Salzburg, Austria, where she saw Percy Lubbock. Writing to Lapsley after she had returned home to Pavillon Colombe, she confessed: "The sound of Time's winged chariot is always with me . . . & there are so many places I want to see & store up!" Soon afterward she was off again on trips that took her to Italy and Scotland. In the middle of these travels she was also working on another novel, *The Buccaneers*, about the misadventures of some American girls from nouveaux riches families who marry into the British aristocracy.

In 1935 a stage dramatization of Edith's novella *The Old Maid* won the Pulitzer Prize. It was quite a triumph for a story that had originally been turned down by almost every major magazine, because the subject matter was considered too controversial. Unfortunately, Edith could not fully enjoy this latest success because her health had lately been declining. The previous spring she had been seriously ill in Italy, and then in April 1935, she suffered a mild stroke. Under the expert care of Elisina Tyler, Edith recovered, however, and was well enough to make a brief trip to Florence. She continued with her writing, and the following summer she made her annual pilgrimage to England. "I wish I knew what people mean when they say they find 'emptiness' in this wonderful adventure of living," she wrote Mary Berenson, "which seems to me to pile up its glories like an horizon-wide sunset as the light declines. I'm afraid I'm an incorrigible life-liver & life-wanderer & adventurer."[4]

Edith celebrated Christmas of 1936 in the same way she had been doing for so many years—at Ste. Claire, in the company of two of her closest friends, Robert Norton and Gaillard Lapsley.

But it was the last such holiday the three companions would enjoy together. Late in the spring of 1937 Edith suffered a serious stroke. Although her devoted friend Elisina Tyler was once again at Edith's bedside, this time she would

not recover. In August, Edith Wharton died at the age of sev-
enty-five. There was a brief ceremony for her at a cemetery in
Versailles, where her friends assembled to pay their last
respects. Then she was buried near the grave of her close
friend and traveling companion, Walter Berry.

16

THE IMMORTALITY OF EDITH WHARTON

In a recent poll of book groups located throughout the country, members were asked to list their favorite titles—fiction as well as nonfiction. Second on the list of popular choices was *The Age of Innocence* by Edith Wharton, the only book that had not been written by a contemporary author. A film version of the novel appeared in 1993, shortly after a screen adaptation of another of Edith's masterpieces, *Ethan Frome*.

What explains the continuing appeal of Edith Wharton's fiction? In part it was her ability to recreate an era that has never lost its interest for us—an era of simpler, surer values that existed before the horrors of two World Wars destroyed it forever. It was also Edith's skill at telling a good story, her sensitive ear for compelling conversation, and keen eye for all the details of a beautiful scene. Above all, Edith Wharton understood people, especially the women of her own social milieu. She clearly recognized the predicament that many of these women faced as they sought to define identities for themselves, achieve some measure of independence, and create an intimate

NOTES

Chapter 1. In Old New York

¹ Allen Churchill, *The Upper Crust: An Informal History of New York's Highest Society* (Englewood Cliffs: Prentice Hall, 1970), 59.

² Louis Auchincloss, ed., *The Hone and Strong Diaries of Old Manhattan* (New York: Abbeville Press, 1989), 197.

³ Edith Wharton, *A Backward Glance* (New York: D. Appleton-Century Company, 1934), 1.

⁴ Ibid., 35.

Chapter 2. Coming of Age

¹ Edith Wharton, *A Backward Glance* (New York: D. Appleton-Century Company, 1934), 73.

² Ibid., 48, 51.

³ Ibid., 57.

⁴ R.W.B. Lewis, *Edith Wharton: A Biography* (New York: Harper & Row, 1975), 24.

⁵ Edith Wharton, *A Backward Glance* (New York: D. Appleton-Century Company, 1934), 95.

Chapter 3. A Writer Emerges

¹ Edith Wharton, "The Fullness of Life" in *The Muse's Tragedy and Other Stories*. Edited by Candace Waid (New York: Signet, 1990), 22–23.

² Edith Wharton, "The Lamp of Psyche" in *The Stories of Edith Wharton*. Selected and introduced by Anita Brookner (New York: Simon & Schuster, 1990), 18.

³ R.W.B. Lewis and Nancy Lewis, eds., *The Letters of Edith Wharton* (New York: Macmillan, 1989), 31.

⁴ Ibid., 32–33.

⁵ Edith Wharton, *A Backward Glance* (New York: D. Appleton-Century Company, 1934), 108.

⁶ Edith Wharton, "Souls Belated" in *The Muse's Tragedy and Other Stories.* Edited by Candace Waid (New York: Signet, 1990), 102.

⁷ Edith Wharton, *A Backward Glance* (New York: D. Appleton-Century Company, 1934), 112.

⁸ Ibid., 113.

⁹ R.W.B. Lewis and Nancy Lewis, eds., *The Letters of Edith Wharton* (New York: Macmillan, 1989), 60.

¹⁰ Edith Wharton, *A Backward Glance* (New York: D. Appleton-Century Company, 1934), 133.

Chapter 4. The Mount

¹ R.W.B. Lewis, *Edith Wharton: A Biography* (New York: Harper & Row, 1975), 101.

² Millicent Bell, *Edith Wharton and Henry James: The Story of Their Friendship* (New York: George Brazillier, 1965), 79.

³ R.W.B. Lewis, *Edith Wharton: A Biography* (New York: Harper & Row, 1975), 160.

⁴ Edith Wharton, *A Backward Glance* (New York: D. Appleton-Century Company, 1934), 172.

⁵ R.W.B. Lewis, *Edith Wharton: A Biography* (New York: Harper & Row, 1975), 127.

⁶ R.W.B. Lewis and Nancy Lewis, eds., *The Letters of Edith Wharton* (New York: Macmillan, 1989), 84.

⁷ Edith Wharton, *A Backward Glance* (New York: D. Appleton-Century Company, 1934), 245.

⁸ Ibid., 249.

⁹ Ibid., 173.

[10] R.W.B. Lewis and Nancy Lewis, eds., *The Letters of Edith Wharton* (New York: Macmillan, 1989), 91.

[11] Edith Wharton, *The Muse's Tragedy and Other Stories.* Edited by Candace Waid (New York: Signet, 1990), 179–80.

[12] Ibid., 199.

[13] Ibid., 200.

[14] Ibid., 211.

Chapter 5. *The House of Mirth*

[1] Edith Wharton, *A Backward Glance* (New York: D. Appleton-Century Company, 1934), 208.

[2] Ibid., 208–9.

[3] Edith Wharton, *The House of Mirth* (New York: New American Library, 1964), 7.

[4] Ibid., 11–12.

[5] Ibid., 69.

[6] Ibid., 72–3.

[7] Ibid., 40–41.

[8] Ibid., 129.

[9] R.W.B. Lewis and Nancy Lewis, eds., *The Letters of Edith Wharton* (New York: Macmillan, 1989), 99.

[10] Edith Wharton, *The House of Mirth* (New York: New American Library, 1964), 184.

[11] Ibid., 196.

[12] Ibid., 267.

[13] Edith Wharton, *A Backward Glance* (New York: D. Appleton-Century Company, 1934), 207.

[14] Edith Wharton, *The House of Mirth* (New York: New American Library, 1964), 311, 319–20.

[15] Ibid., 319.

Chapter 6. Teddy Wharton and Morton Fullerton

¹ R.W.B. Lewis, *Edith Wharton: A Biography* (New York: Harper & Row, 1975), 192.

² R.W.B. Lewis and Nancy Lewis, eds., *The Letters of Edith Wharton* (New York: Macmillan, 1989), 130.

³ Millicent Bell, *Edith Wharton and Henry James: The Story of Their Friendship* (New York: George Brazillier, 1965), 158–9.

⁴ Ibid., 159–160.

⁵ R.W.B. Lewis and Nancy Lewis, eds., *The Letters of Edith Wharton* (New York: Macmillan, 1989), 134–5.

⁶ Ibid., 145.

⁷ Ibid., 160.

⁸ Ibid., 189.

⁹ Ibid., 215.

¹⁰ Ibid., 218.

Chapter 7. *Ethan Frome*

¹ Edith Wharton, *A Backward Glance* (New York: D. Appleton-Century Company, 1934), 293–4.

² Edith Wharton, *Ethan Frome* (New York: Macmillan, 1987), 1.

³ Ibid., 97.

⁴ Ibid., 13.

⁵ Ibid., 52.

⁶ Ibid., 36.

⁷ Ibid., 59.

⁸ Ibid., 66.

⁹ Ibid., 70.

¹⁰ Ibid., 85.

Chapter 8. Endings and Beginnings
    [1] Edith Wharton, *The Muse's Tragedy and Other Stories.* Edited by Candace Waid (New York: Signet, 1990), 408.
    [2] Ibid., 427.
    [3] R.W.B. Lewis and Nancy Lewis, eds., *The Letters of Edith Wharton* (New York: Macmillan, 1989), 289.

Chapter 9. *The Reef*
    [1] Edith Wharton, *The Reef* (New York: Scribner's, 1965), 314.
    [2] Ibid., 88.
    [3] Ibid., 93.
    [4] Ibid., 107.
    [5] Ibid., 172.
    [6] Ibid., 299–300.
    [7] R.W.B. Lewis, *Edith Wharton: A Biography* (New York: Harper & Row, 1975), 325–6.
    [8] Edith Wharton, *The Reef* (New York: Scribner's, 1965), 322.

Chapter 10. *The Custom of the Country*
    [1] Edith Wharton, *The Custom of the Country* (New York: Bantam, 1991), 47.
    [2] Ibid., 49.
    [3] Ibid., 3–4.
    [4] Ibid., 344.
    [5] Ibid., 105.
    [6] Ibid., 228.
    [7] Ibid., 223.
    [8] Ibid., 347.
    [9] Ibid., 376.

Chapter 11. War!

[1] R.W.B. Lewis and Nancy Lewis, eds., *The Letters of Edith Wharton* (New York: Macmillan, 1989), 286.

[2] Ibid., 312–3.

[3] Edith Wharton, *A Backward Glance* (New York: D. Appleton-Century Company, 1934), 338.

[4] R.W.B. Lewis, *Edith Wharton: A Biography* (New York: Harper & Row, 1975), 384.

[5] R.W.B. Lewis and Nancy Lewis, eds., *The Letters of Edith Wharton* (New York: Macmillan, 1989), 382–3.

[6] Ibid., 349.

[7] Ibid., 351.

[8] Edith Wharton, *A Backward Glance* (New York: D. Appleton-Century Company, 1934), 356–7.

Chapter 12. *The Age of Innocence*

[1] Edith Wharton, *A Backward Glance* (New York: D. Appleton-Century Company, 1934), 369.

[2] R.W.B. Lewis and Nancy Lewis, eds., *The Letters of Edith Wharton* (New York: Macmillan, 1989), 445.

[3] Edith Wharton, *The Age of Innocence* (New York: Macmillan, 1986), 41.

[4] Ibid., 73.

[5] Ibid., 76.

[6] Ibid., 195.

[7] Ibid., 237–8.

[8] Ibid., 290–1.

[9] Ibid., 334.

Chapter 13. Transitions and the Writer's Art
    [1] R.W.B. Lewis, *Edith Wharton: A Biography* (New York: Harper & Row, 1975), 421.
    [2] R.W.B. Lewis and Nancy Lewis, eds., *The Letters of Edith Wharton* (New York: Macmillan, 1989), 503.
    [3] Ibid., 504.
    [4] Edith Wharton, *Twilight Sleep* (New York: D. Appleton-Century Company, 1927), 3–4.
    [5] Ibid., 189.
    [6] Ibid., 33.
    [7] Edith Wharton, *Old New York* (New York: D. Appleton-Century Company, 1924), 182–3.
    [8] Margaret B. McDowell, *Edith Wharton* (Boston: Twayne Publishers, 1976), 84.
    [9] Edith Wharton, *The Selected Short Stories* (New York: Scribner's, 1991), 350.
    [10] Ibid., 352.

Chapter 14. *Hudson River Bracketed*
    [1] R.W.B. Lewis and Nancy Lewis, eds., *The Letters of Edith Wharton* (New York: Macmillan, 1989), 525.
    [2] Edith Wharton, *Hudson River Bracketed* (New York: D. Appleton-Century Company, 1929), 6.
    [3] Ibid., 41.
    [4] Ibid., 56.
    [5] Ibid., 276, 320, 401.
    [6] Ibid., 292, 294.
    [7] Ibid., 326.
    [8] Ibid., 409.
    [9] Ibid., 536.

Chapter 15. The Final Years

     [1] R.W.B. Lewis and Nancy Lewis, eds., *The Letters of Edith Wharton* (New York: Macmillan, 1989), 522.

     [2] Ibid., 559–60.

     [3] Ibid., 532.

     [4] Ibid., 569.

     [5] Ibid., 598.

CHRONOLOGY

1861	Civil War breaks out
1862	Edith Newbold Jones born in New York City
1865	Civil War ends: the Joneses move to Europe
1885	Edith marries Edward Robbins (Teddy) Wharton
1891	*Scribner's* magazine publishes *Mrs. Mantsey's View*
1899	Scribner's publishes Edith's first book of fiction, *The Greater Inclination*
1902	Edith moves to The Mount, her home in Lenox, Massachusetts; her first novel, *The Valley of Decision*, is published
1905	*The House of Mirth* is published and soon becomes America's best-selling novel
1907	Edith takes up residence in Paris; she meets Morton Fullerton
1911	*Ethan Frome* is published; Edith leaves The Mount
1913	Edith divorces Teddy Wharton; *The Custom of the Country* is published
1914	World War I breaks out in Europe; Edith organizes relief for refugees, children and soldiers
1918	World War I ends
1920	*The Age of Innocence* is published
1921	Edith is awarded the Pulitzer Prize
1929	*Hudson River Bracketed* is published
1937	Edith Wharton dies in France

FURTHER READING

Auchincloss, Louis, ed. *The Hone and Strong Diaries of Old Manhattan.* New York: Abbeville Press, 1989.

Auchincloss, Louis. *Edith Wharton: A Woman in Her Time.* New York: Viking, 1971.

Bairiati, Elonora, et al. *La Belle Epoque: Fifteen Europhoric Years of European History.* New York: William Morrow, 1978.

Bell, Millicent. *Edith Wharton and Henry James: The Story of Their Friendship.* New York: George Brazillier, 1965.

Bloom, Harold, ed. *Edith Wharton.* New York: Chelsea House, 1986.

Churchill, Allen. *The Upper Crust: An Informal History of New York's Highest Society.* Englewood Cliffs: Prentice Hall, 1970.

Lewis, R.W.B. *Edith Wharton: A Biography.* New York: Harper & Row, 1975.

Lewis, R.W.B. and Nancy Lewis, eds. *The Letters of Edith Wharton.* New York: Macmillan, 1989.

McDowell, Margaret. *Edith Wharton.* Boston: Twayne Publishers, 1976.

Priestly, J.B. *The Edwardians.* New York: Harper & Row, 1978.

Tuchman, Barbara. *The Guns of August.* New York: Bantam, 1989.

Tuchman, Barbara. *The Proud Tower.* New York: Bantam, 1989.

Wharton, Edith. *The Age of Innocence.* New York: Macmillan, 1986.

Wharton, Edith. *A Backward Glance.* New York: D. Appleton-Century Company, 1934.

Wharton, Edith. *The Custom of the Country.* New York: Bantam, 1991.

Wharton, Edith. *Ethan Frome.* New York: Macmillan, 1987.

Wharton, Edith. *The House of Mirth.* New York: New American Library, 1964.

Wharton, Edith. *Hudson River Bracketed.* New York: Scribner's, 1957.

Wharton, Edith. *Madame de Treymes and Others.* London: Virago Press, 1984.

Wharton, Edith. *The Muse's Tragedy and Other Stories.* New York: Signet, 1990.

Wharton, Edith. *Old New York.* New York: D. Appleton-Century Company, 1924.

Wharton, Edith. *The Reef.* New York: Scribner's, 1965.

Wharton, Edith. *The Selected Short Stories of Edith Wharton.* New York: Scribner's, 1991.

Wharton, Edith. *The Stories of Edith Wharton.* New York: Simon & Schuster, 1990.

Wharton, Edith. *Twilight Sleep.* New York: D. Appleton-Century Company, 1927.

INDEX

A

Academy of Music (New York City), 2, 5
Adams, Brooks, 34
Adams, Henry, 58
After Holbein (short story), 130
Age of Innocence, The (novel), 101–9, 111, 117, 124, 133
Alhambra (Spain), 8, 9
Algiers, 92
American, The (James), 34
American Hostels for Refugees, 94
American Revolution, 6
Appleton (publisher), 113, 117, 128
archery, 11
Ascot (England), 74
Astor, Caroline Schermerhorn, 15–17
Astor, John Jacob, 15
Astor, Nancy (Lady Astor), 74
Astor, Waldorf (2nd Viscount Astor), 74
Astor, William Backhouse, 15
Atlantic Monthly (magazine), 12, 34, 63
Austria, 130
automobiles, 36, 38, 54, 58
Autre Temps . . . (short story), 71–72

B

Backward Glance, A (autobiography), 7, 28, 34, 36–37, 81, 102, 127, 128, 135
balls, 2, 16–17, 74
Bar Harbor (Maine), 18
Belgium, refugee children from, 95
Belmont, August, 15
Berenson, Bernard, 112
Berenson, Mary, 131
Bergamo (Italy), 114

Berkshires, the. *See* Mount, the (Lenox).
Berry, Walter Van Rensselaer
    death of, 114
    as Edith's editor, 26–28, 102
    friendship of Edith and, 34, 73, 92–93, 95, 97, 98, 112, 132
    meeting of Edith and, 18
    boating in Central Park (New York City), 4–5
Bodiam Castle (England), 37, 127
Boston (Massachusetts), 72, 94
Bourget, Minnie, 29, 30, 97, 112
Bourget, Paul, 29, 30, 53, 97, 112
Broadway (New York City), 1, 3
Brownell, William Crary, 38
Buccaneers, The (novel), 131
Bunker Hill, battle of, 6
Burlingame, Edward, 25, 43–44

C

Castle Garden (New York City), 2–3
Central Park (New York City), 4–5, 15
Century magazine, 19
Children of Flanders Rescue Committee, 95
Civil War, 7, 15
Cliveden (country house in England), 74
Codman, Ogden, 23, 26
Columbia University, 83, 102
coming-out parties, 14
Confession (short story), 130
Custom of the Country, The (novel), 81–89, 92, 101
    serial rights for, 81
Cutting, Bayard, 23

D

Daisy Miller (James), 34
Decoration of Houses, The (book),
    26–27
de Fitz-James, Rosa, 112
Delmonico's restaurant (New York
    City), 14
Derby, the, 74
Dickens, Charles, 2
dinner parties, 5, 16, 74
divorce, 38–39, 82, 83, 92
    Edith's, 72, 74
Duration (short story), 130

E

Edith Wharton Committees, 94
Edward VII (when Prince of Wales),
    1–2
England, 17, 29, 30, 35–37, 53, 73,
    74, 94, 127
Ethan Frome (novel), 64–69, 75, 98,
    133
Expiation (short story), 40–41
Eyes, The (short story), 63

F

Fast and Loose (novella), 40–41
Fifth Avenue (New York City), 3, 7,
    15
Fifth Avenue Hotel (New York City),
    2
*Fighting France, from Dunkerque to
    Belfort* (book), 97
Fitzgerald, F. Scott, 113
Fitz-James, Rosa de, 112
flashbacks, 63, 75–76
Florence (Italy), 9, 25, 73, 131
Forty-second Street reservoir (New
    York City), 7
400, the (New York City), 16

France
    clash of American culture with that
        of, 81–83, 88–89
    Edith's apartment in, 53–54, 56–58,
        64, 73, 81–82, 111
    Edith's later homes in, 111–13, 131
    Edith's parents in, 6, 9, 17
    Edith's travels in, 36, 74
    in World War I, 92–99
Franz Ferdinand, Archduke, 92–93
Fullerton, Morton, 54, 58–61, 65, 73,
    97
Fullness of Life, The (short story),
    21–23

G

Gide, André, 94, 97, 112
Glimpses of the Moon, The (novel), 113
Gods Arrive, The (novel), 127–28
Golden Bowl, The (James), 79
Grant, Robert, 34
Great Depression, the, 128
Greater Inclination, The (short stories),
    28, 34–35
Greece, 114
Gross, Catherine, 130

H

Hardy, Thomas, 35
Harper's magazine, 19
Harvard University, 30, 83
Hot Springs (Arkansas), 57, 58
House of Mirth, The (novel), 43–53,
    65, 69, 84
    central theme of, 51
    popularity of, 44
Hudson River Bracketed (novel),
    121–26, 127
Hunt, Richard Morris, 48
Hyères (France), 111

I

immigration into the United States, 3
Irving, Washington, 9, 14
Italy, 8, 9, 19, 25, 29, 30, 43, 73, 74, 114, 131

J

James, Henry
    advises Edith to "Do New York," 35–36, 43
    death of, 97
    Edith's fiction compared to that of, 38
    first meeting of Edith and, 34–35
    friendship between Edith and, 37–38, 54, 57, 63, 72–74, 127, 134
    gift from Edith to, 91
    praise of Edith's works by, 68, 79
    World War I letters from Edith to, 95–97
Jerome, Leonard, 15
Jewett, Rutger, 128, 129
Jones, Beatrix, 92
Jones, Edith Newbold. See Wharton, Edith.
Jones, Elizabeth Schermerhorn, 6
Jones, Freddy, 92
Jones, George Frederic, 6–9, 12–14, 17
Jones, Joshua, 32
Jones, Lucretia Rhinelander, 6–9, 12–15
Jones, Mary Cadwalader (Minnie), 92, 128, 130, 134

K

Knickerbocker Club (New York City), 4

L

Ladies Home Journal (magazine), 128
Lamb House (James's home in England), 36–37
Lamp of Psyche, The (short story), 23–24
Land's End (Newport home), 26
landscape gardening, 111–12
Lapsley, Gaillard, 34, 74, 97, 114, 130, 131, 134
Last Asset, The (short story), 54
Legion of Honor, 97
Lenox (Massachusetts). *See* Mount, the.
Lewis, R. W. B., 18, 56
Lewis, Sinclair, 102
Lincoln, Abraham, 7
Lind, Jenny, 2
Lodge, Bay, 34
Lodge, Henry Cabot, 34
London (England), 17, 29, 35, 36, 53, 73, 74
Longfellow, Henry Wadsworth, 12
Louis Philippe (king of France), 6
Lubbock, Percy, 94, 97, 130

M

McAllister, Ward, 16
McDowell, Margaret, 118
Madame de Treymes (novella), 54
Madison Avenue (New York City), 15, 19
Madison Square (New York City), 4
Main Street (Lewis), 102
Manhattan Club (New York City), 4
Mantua (Italy), 73
Marne, first battle of the, 92
Marseillaise, the, 93
Middle West, 102, 121
Minturn, Robert, 23

Morton, Mrs. Levi, 14
Motor Flight Through France, A (book), 63
Mount, the (Lenox home), 31–34, 38, 43, 56, 57–59, 64, 72–73, 111
  sale of, 73
Mount, the (Long Island home), 6
Mrs. Manstey's View (short story), 19
Muse's Tragedy, The (short story), 27

N

Newport (Rhode Island)
  crass materialism of, 31
  Edith's poetry printed in, 12
  Land's End home in, 26
  Pencraig estate at, 7, 11, 18, 19, 23
  Teddy returns to, 31
New York City. *See also specific places.*
  Edith Wharton Committee in, 94
  1860 population of, 3
  European connections of, 2–3
  harbor of, 3
  illustration of homes of, 48
  nouveaux riches in, 15, 48, 83
  old families of, 4, 6, 15, 82–83
  opera in, 2, 5, 103
  Prince of Wales in, 1–2
  rents as source of old fortunes of, 4, 7
New York Stock Exchange, 3
New York Times, 97
Noailles, Comtesse Anna de, 53
Nobel Prize, 72
North Africa, 92
Norton, Charles Eliot, 30, 38, 57, 59
Norton, Robert, 111, 114, 127, 131, 134
Norton, Sara, 30, 57, 59, 91, 94, 134

O

Old Maid, The (novella), 117–18
  stage dramatization of, 131
Old New York (four novellas), 117–18
Olmsted, Frederick Law, 4
Other Two, The (short story), 38–40

P

Paris (France)
  Edith's apartment in, 53–54, 56–58, 64, 73, 81–82, 111
  Edith's parents in, 6, 9
  in World War I, 92–94, 97–98
Parma (Italy), 73
Pavillon Colombe (home in France), 111–13, 131
Pelican, The (short story), 27
Pencraig (Newport estate), 7, 11, 18, 19, 23
Perry, Caroline Slidell, 15
Perry, Matthew, 15
Perry, Oliver Hazard, 15
Philadelphia, 94
Poe, Edgar Allan, 63
Pomegranate Seed (short story), 129
Portrait of a Lady (James), 34
Prince of Wales (future Edward VII), 1–2
Pulitzer Prize, 102, 112, 131

R

Reef, The (novel), 75–81
refugees in World War I, 94–95
Rhinelander family, 6
Robinson, Edward, 34
Roman Fever (short story), 119–20
Rome (Italy), 8, 43
Rye (England), 36

S

Ste. Claire (home in France), 111–12, 114, 131
Salzburg (Austria), 130
Sarajevo (Bosnia), 93
Saratoga, battle of, 6
Sargent, John Singer, 35
Schermerhorn, Caroline. *See* Astor, Caroline Schermerhorn.
Scribner, Charles, 58, 81, 91
Scribner's magazine, 19, 21, 23, 25, 29, 43–44, 68, 81, 97
Scribner's publishing house, 27–29, 44, 63, 113
Seville (Spain), 8–9
Smith, John Hugh, 113, 134
Son at the Front, A (novel), 113, 117
Souls Belated (short story), 27–28
Spain, 8–9, 92
stage dramatization of *The Old Maid*, 131
Stevens, Ebenezer, 6, 31
Stevens, Harry, 18
Stevens, Mrs. Paran, 18
Strong, Edward Templeton, 1, 2
Summer (novella), 98
summer life
  in Central Park (New York City), 4–5
  in Newport, 11, 18
Switzerland, 29, 60

T

Tales of Men and Ghosts (book of ghost stories), 63
Teddy. *See* Wharton, Edward Robinson (Teddy).
Temperate Zone, The (short story), 119

Touchstone, The (novella), 29–30
Trevelyan, George, 35
Trinity Church (New York City), 2
Tunis, 92
Twilight Sleep (novel), 115–17
Tyler, Elisina, 94–95, 97, 121, 131, 134
Tyler, Royall, 94–95, 97, 111
Tyler, William, 95

U

Union League Club (New York City), 4

V

Valley of Decision, The (novel), 30, 31, 35, 56
Vanderbilt, Cornelius, 15
Vaux, Calvert, 4
Venice (Italy), 114
Verona (Italy), 73

W

Wall Street (New York City), 3
Washington Square (New York City), 3, 34, 101
Wharton, Edith
  autobiography of, 7, 28, 34, 36–37, 81, 102, 127, 128, 135
  birth and childhood of, 7–12
  childlessness of, 54
  continuing appeal of fiction of, 133–34
  death of, 131–32
  descriptions of, 7, 14
  divorce of, 72, 74
  early writings of, 11–12
  friendships of, 91, 134–35
  ghost stories of, 63

Wharton, Edith (*continued*)
    honorary degree to, 113
    independent income of, 32, 56–57,
        72–73, 113, 134
    Legion of Honor awarded to, 97
    love affair of, 54, 58–61
    marriage of, 18–19. *See also*
        Wharton, Edward Robbins
        (Teddy).
    nervous breakdown of, 25–26
    novels of. *See specific novels by name.*
    poetry of, 12, 19
    Pulitzer Prize to, 102, 112, 131
    short stories of, 19, 21–25, 27–28,
        38–41, 54, 71–72, 117–20,
        128–30
    small dogs as pets of, 33, 54
    travel articles of, 29
    World War I activities of, 93–99,
        113, 135
    on writing fiction, 118, 135
    as young debutante, 14, 16–19

Wharton, Edward Robbins (Teddy)
    breakdown of marriage of, 54–60,
        72–74
    marriage of Edith and, 18–19
    married life of, 23, 26, 29–33, 36,
        43, 65, 114
    nervous collapse of, 56–57
Wilson, Woodrow, 98
winter sports in New York City, 5
Winthrop, Egerton, 19, 23, 34, 58, 91
World War I, 92–99, 101, 113, 135
    Edith's description of battles of,
        95–97
    U.S. entry into, 98
Worth of Paris (jewelers), 17
Writing of Fiction, The (book), 118

Y

Yale University, 113
Yorktown, battle of, 6